FREE
TO
BE ME

A GUIDE TO
BIBLICAL SECURITY

By

Charles T. Bordonaro

Beacon Light Publishing, Inc.
P.O. Box 1612
Thousand Oaks, CA 91358

FREE TO BE ME
A Guide To
Biblical Security

By
Charles T. Bordonaro

SAN: 299-6952
Beacon Light Publishing, Inc.
P.O. Box 1612
Thousand Oaks, CA 91358

Copyright © 1998 Charles T. Bordonaro
First Edition

Printed in the United States of America

Unless otherwise indicated, Bible verses quoted in this book are from THE NEW AMERICAN STANDARD BIBLE. Copyright © The Lockman Foundation 1960, 1962, 1963, 1968, 1971, 1972, 1973, 1975, 1977, 1988.

Lighthouse Illustrations: Lynda K. Keena
Cover Design: Lynda K. Keena
Cover Art Director: Jon Osmundsen

Library of Congress Catalog Card Number: 98-93501
ISBN: 1-892810-11-5

Acknowledgments

A book like this cannot find its way into the publisher's hands except through the valuable help of many people. My good friend and fellow Christian servant, Thomas J. Meade, Ph.D., aided in guiding the flow and expressions of the thoughts within the book. Dr. Meade is professor of chemistry and biology at California Institute of Technology, Pasadena, CA.

Betty L. Sulahian, a member of Trinity Baptist Church and a retired English teacher, gave needed advice, encouragement, and constructive criticism.

Lynda K. Keena, literary consultant and producer of "Amazing Biographies," a cable TV program, edited grammar, punctuation, spelling, and sentence structure. Lynda also designed the book cover.

Paul Keena, French language instructor, tutor, translator and interpreter, added valuable comments and suggestions regarding the content of the manuscript.

Former pastor and dear friend, Ron Kobler, also gave needed viewpoints regarding the doctrinal content of the book.

I would not have been able to begin nor complete the monumental task of writing *Free To Be Me* without the tireless support and encouragement I received from many others. God has placed my wife, Donna, my children, and other Christians before me as a testimony of God's gracious provisions. Watching people grow in the security of the Lord has been a continuous joy and inspiration to me.

Finally, I am grateful to God for the security He has given to me in the Lord Jesus Christ. When I began the life of peace and joy in Christ on August 16, 1966, I did not realize that God would make me more secure. I praise Him for His omnipotent hand, with which He has held me.

SAFE AND SECURE

Oh, the joy of freedom ringing loud and clear!
Walking through life securely, having no fear.

For God hath said He would always bring cheer,
To the one who realizes that He's always near.

Quickly come to the Lord! To the Savior so great.
There's not a moment to lose. You must not wait!

Into His loving arms, rest with joy sublime.
He'll keep you safe forever, 'til the end of time.

Time goes on. Years pass and God is not heeded.
As we foolishly live for things that are not needed.

Not one day must pass, not one moment to lose.
Turn to the Lord. In Him there's real life to choose!

He'll be with you, holding you close to His breast.
And bring you safely to heaven for eternity's rest.

Safe and secure, we'll be at home in heaven at last.
For the trials of earth will soon all be in the past.

But while we wait for the bliss of eternity's hour,
We are secure today, kept by His mighty power.

Safe and secure in heaven throughout eternity's day.
Safe and secure on earth, walking with Christ alway.

C.T.B.

TABLE OF CONTENTS

PREFACE

Free To Be Me is not an expression of rebellion against God's divine ownership of believers. All Christians have been bought by the precious blood of Christ, and thus, belong to God (I Corinthians 6:19,20). The biblical freedom expressed in the following pages cannot be separated from the position the believer has in Christ. There is no other true freedom for anyone. Apart from Christ, people do not have the security to freely be themselves before God. In Christ, the Christian can face life confidently without the confusing bondage of fear, anxiety, and vanity.

The purpose of the book, *Free To Be Me*, is to present biblical truths which lead people into a life of practical security. It is intended to be a practical and theological handbook for the believer. It is a book which shows how Bible teachings fit into everyday life in a vibrant and practical way.

A pair of pants hanging in the closet is good. Yet, it is not until the pants are put on and worn do they serve the purpose for which they were made. Practical theology has the same intent: to show how to use Bible teaching the way God intended it to be used.

Doctrines can often be represented as isolated concepts. When Bible teachings are made to stand as "islands," confusion may be the consequence. When Bible truths are integrated, believed, and followed, the result will bring joyful security.

Jesus Christ taught that people would be set free, that is, if they trusted Him (the Truth). Christ was not talking about isolated teachings of Bible doctrines. He would have been referring to *all* the concepts of truth. Such concepts *must not* contradict one another.

Isolated teachings can be contradicting, thus leading to confusion. Truth must be successfully viewed as a unit, thus giving a complete picture for one's understanding.

Our modern society is insecure and confused. Many churches, religions, employers, teachers, friends, relatives, and acquaintances have become trapped by isolated teachings. This is manifested by the confusion of insecure lifestyles.

Bondage caused by fear and insecurity can be experienced when one or more teachings are isolated from known truths. However, freedom is attained by systematically integrating concepts of truth together.

These writings are not intended to be a study in psychology. They are intended to be a study of practical biblical security. However, the attainment of biblical security may result in psychological changes.

While considering the truths of the Scriptures, salvation by grace through faith will also be addressed. *Free To Be Me* is not intended to be a book about salvation. However, it is not possible to deal with the subject of security without addressing the primary cornerstone of the Christian faith -- salvation by faith alone in the Lord Jesus Christ.

The teachings of security from the Bible will be related to our past, our present, and our future in this book. While these may not be "new" truths, *"Free To Be Me"* places them together in a new and practical way. The purpose in placing these truths together is to give a complete picture of a peaceful secure life. Thus, my hope is to lead people away from error. Living in error never gives birth to freedom and security. Freedom and security are the results of tying truths together and responding positively to those truths.

Faith in God and acceptance by Him make up the

basic argument for security. From this base, the principles of security cause a person to live in freedom. Security enables the believer to become the kind of person God desires him to be as an individual.

Most people live in fear of what others may think of them. Driven by opinions, rather than by truth, will always undermine personal freedom and security. Opinions change. Truth does not change. Truth is always true and always has been true and always will be true. This being the case, one would be foolish to build his life on opinions. Yet, many people do just that! Opinions and traditions will not allow freedom and security to be the governing principles of life.

Free To Be Me offers the reader a path into the life of freedom and security promised by the Lord Jesus Christ. It ties biblical truths together and promotes freedom from bondage and confusion. This book relates freedom and security to practical areas of life such as marriage, family, parents, employment, peer pressure, friendships, and religion.

My hope is that this book will help relieve the unnecessary pain in believers' hearts caused by the fallacy of following opinions and traditions. It is my desire to see the pain replaced with the freedom and security offered by the Lord Jesus Christ. It is my prayer that God will use this book as a tool in the hands of God's people to help develop security as a lifestyle.

C.T.B. 1998

FREE TO BE ME

A Guide To Biblical Security

Introduction

The main purpose of this book is to provide every reader with the opportunity to be secure with God. God is the only One Who can give the necessary security, enabling people to be free to be themselves.

Are you happy and secure in life? Does the abundant, full, secure life that Jesus spoke seem like a myth to you? In John 10:10, Christ tells us, " ... I came that they might have life, and might have it abundantly." Is this purpose statement from Christ a genuine offer? Are abundant joy and security attainable? Or, is security the proverbial carrot dangling in front of the donkey just to get him to pull a cart? Is personal security a promise with no possible fulfillment?

Do your knowledge of God and faith in God cause you to be secure in Him? Or, have your knowledge and faith become mere religious and ceremonial practices without depth or meaning? Is security a lifestyle for you? Or, is it an abstract theory?

These and other questions will be answered in this

1

book. It is my desire to make available to the reader a text with the tools necessary to possess and to develop genuine security as an everyday lifestyle.

Security is a huge topic. It effects every person from every background. It is sought after with great passion and diligence. With security, all people are equal before God. It is the great leveler of mankind. Our nation has recognized that the freedom of the United States rests upon the security of the people. If there is constant fear of other nations conquering the USA, the citizens would not be able to boast of nor experience their freedom. The citizens of the United States are free to be the kind of people they desire to be, under the rules and regulations of the government.

This is also true of Christians. If they are not secure in Christ, they will not have the freedom to be themselves before God. They will lack freedom to be the kind of people they should be under Christ's supervision.

Unfortunately, there are citizens of the United States who have abused their freedoms. They have expressed their freedom in ways which trespass against the laws of their country and against the common decency of others. Liberty is not permission to be offensive and abusive to others.

So also, freedom in Christ is not a license to break God's commandments. Freedom does not give the Christian the right to treat others offensively. The liberty caused by the believer's security in Christ is to be expressed under the canopy of God's divine leadership.

Wars are fought for "security." Men and women have laid down their very lives for the security of their countries. The relationship between security and freedom is clearly seen.

Job security is desired in every place of employment. Financial independence, as one approaches retirement, is a dream that has boosted the sale of stocks, and mutual funds everywhere. The business of selling annuities and life insurance policies continues to prosper.

Psychologists' businesses are doing very well. Their proclaimed goal is to help people gain security in life. Cosmetology and medicine are markets that are booming. The attempt is to make people look secure and feel accepted. Security has become a multi-billion dollar business. Yet, people are not secure.

People without security are certainly miserable and very confused. Anxiety, fear, loss, anger, disappointment, and loneliness are ruling characteristics over all those who have no security. These conditions are caused by seeking the right thing in the wrong places and in the wrong ways. "If I only had a friend," and "Can't we all get along?", are songs sung and questions asked. This is symptomatic of deep problems lying within the heart of man.

There is inequity in the attainment of security. One person may come from a broken home with a poverty-stricken background with abuse, hatred, and unhappiness. Another person may come from a two-parent home of wealth, education, and relative happiness. The person from the broken home may blossom into a bold and confident person. He portrays all the characteristics of love, kindness, and security. On the other hand, the person with the fine upbringing may end up homeless, fearful, and insecure.

Insecurity brings people into bondage. Fear, selfishness, and pride are aspects of bondage caused by insecurity. God-given security sets a person free to be himself. A secure person does not have to become someone else to find joy and purpose in living. God has a design for each person. He desires people to be the kinds of persons that *He* wants them to be. Freedom to face life, its trials and joys, will be the result for all those who trust God.

The basis for security can be found only in God through the person of the Lord Jesus Christ. Security is a lifestyle to be entered into with God. There must be more to life than material things, employment, education, friends, family, and religion.

Living in security ought to be the goal of all true believers in the Lord Jesus Christ. May God be glorified as we become secure in His matchless love, mercy, and grace.

Chapter 1

Security Defined

Healthy souls, how can it be, in this dark world of sin?
For Jesus came, His blood to shed, to cleanse us all within.
Living life, so all alone, outside God's Wondrous plan,
God's work of grace is all forgot, by the mind of sinful man.

Security is reliability. Reliability is tested by
pressure, force, and stress. It is characterized by the
faithfulness of strength, firmness, soundness,
steadiness, and stability. Tension, stress, difficulties,
and trials test the authenticity of security.

Security is experienced when one knows that all is well
even when all is not well. When people are tried and
tested, they will be found to be reliable and stable, or
unreliable and unstable. If they are not sure that all is
well during trials and tests, they may become insecure.
If they know that all *is* well during times of adversity,
they may maintain a secure lifestyle. A secure person
is one who is reliable, especially during times of
difficulty.

Stability can only be entered into by people with a
sense of belonging, a sense of family, a sense of
community, and a sense of roots and heritage. How

does one fit into this world of God's making? Are people here by chance? Does man really belong here? What is the purpose of man's existence upon this planet? Is there an end to all that he is involved in?

The answers to these questions, and the answers necessary to possess an abundant life are found in the security one experiences in God. Only in Him does one find the reason for his existence and his heritage. When God is trusted, He gives security and purpose to the believer.

Psychology is reported to be concerned with the wellness of the soul. The Bible certainly is:

Isaiah 1:5,6 -- "Where will you be stricken again, As you continue in your rebellion? The whole head is sick, And the whole heart is faint. From the sole of the foot even to the head There is nothing sound in it, Only bruises, welts, and raw wounds, Not pressed out or bandaged, Nor softened with oil."

The picture drawn by the prophet Isaiah is one of ill health. The heart of rebellious man is described as sickness before the Lord. Man's head, heart, and everything else from his toes to his scalp have been affected by sin. The result is not health, but the exact opposite. Sickness has never been the picture of security. Sickness portrays weakness, inability, and death.

It is a familiar statement to hear someone say that another person is insecure. What do they mean by that? Usually, they are talking about certain characteristics that they have noticed in that person's life: they have trouble making decisions; they don't stick to a particular plan after they have made a decision; they have difficulty keeping commitments;

they are fearful of taking a stand; they don't know where their path is taking them; they lack confidence even in the things they do well; they live a constant approval-seeking life.

If this is true of insecurity, the opposite would be true of security. Secure people make decisions and follow through with commitment. They are not fearful of life. They know where they are going and they manifest it through a confident lifestyle. Approval or disapproval of their lives and of their decisions by others is not the chief goal of their lives.

The Soul of Man

Sick heads, faint hearts, and unhealthy spiritual lives are mentioned in the above passage from Isaiah. These sound like severe psychological problems, and indeed they are! Man's problem is a sick soul.

In fact, the New Testament declares that man is spiritually dead, separated from God (Ephesians 2:1; Romans 5:12). He is mortally wounded and is continuously oppressed by sin. Without Christ, his only choice is to continue living as a wounded, unhealthy creature. His soul is not well. Therefore, his life is not secure (reliable).

In order to have security, man must make sure his soul is in a right relationship with His Creator. He must make sure that his mortal sinful wounds are healed. As noted in Isaiah 1:5,6, insecurity is defined from this spiritual point of view.

From the New Testament Greek word for "soul", we get the transliterated word, "psyche." Psychology is the study of the psyche, or the study of the soul. In the Bible, it is sometimes translated "life." Jesus Christ laid down His life (psyche -- soul) for us.

When God breathed into man's nostrils the breath of life, man became a living life ("soul" -- Genesis 2:7). When Adam sinned, he died. His soul (life) became separated from God. He became insecure. His life was no longer spiritually attached to his Creator, his only foundation of security. By sinning, he set himself apart from God. Sin, man's first and foremost enemy, severed man from his best friend, God.

God is the Creator of man's soul. One must turn to the Maker of the soul in order to obtain a proper understanding of the soul's condition. God has made the rules whereby man's soul can be maintained in spiritual health. Peace and security from the Lord are essential to the well-being of the life and soul of every individual.

Security affects how people feel, their outlook in life, how they treat others, what their perspective is regarding the world, how they view possessions or lack of them, and how they perceive their own needs. When the soul of man is secure in relationship to God, man's outlook, feelings, behavior, and attitudes will reflect that security.

Security is a principle based upon foundations. God tells us in His Word (I Corinthians 3:11) that there is no foundation other than the Lord Jesus Christ. Other felt or perceived foundations would then be classified as false foundations. Whatever man has become founded upon (rooted and grounded in) will be the determining factor of his security. Becoming rooted and grounded in false foundations can only bring false security. Woe to the one whose foundation is not Christ. Christ is the Eternal Rock of Ages, the only true immovable foundation.

God constantly reminds His creation that He is the Rock. Note the personal possessive pronouns written in the first person singular in Psalm 18:2 -- "The Lord is *my* rock and *my* fortress and *my* deliverer, *My* God, *my* rock, in whom I take refuge; *My* shield and the horn of *my* salvation, *my* stronghold." (Italics -- mine).

Security is obviously a personal possession by those who have the "Rock." This is not the way that many people look at life. Most people feel that earthly possessions cause security. The Bible teaches that God, Who is our personal possession, *is* security.

Four Enemies of Security

Four enemies have invaded the realm of God's intended purposes as to how He has represented Himself to Mankind. While more may be listed, these enemies comprise a general list. Other enemies can easily be placed under these four general headings. These four general categories of enemies are: Atheism, Agnosticism, Gnosticism, and Humanism.

Atheism

Atheism denies the very existence of God. Therefore, it denies that God is the immovable and unchanging Rock. Refusing to recognize the existence of God does not make God cease to exist. However, atheism *does* cause man's thinking to be placed on a foundation other than the One Who is immovable. If man's thoughts tell him there is no God, his thoughts also tell him that there is no security. Psalm 71:1 says, "In thee, O Lord, do I put my trust: let me never be put to confusion" (KJV). One cannot trust God if one does not believe that God truly exists. Confusion is the chief result of atheism. Confusion is *never* security.

There has been in recent times a promoted desire for adopted children to find their biological parents. They yearn for an identity, hoping for a foundation and a heritage to be established, adding to their security. Until they find who their parents are, they may not feel as if they belong. They lack the sense of family and community. Imagine lying to an adopted child, telling him that his biological parents never existed!

Atheism offers the same insecure cruelty to mankind. Atheism robs people of the opportunity to have the sense that they belong to the Heavenly Father, the One Who made them.

Atheism offers no real foundation. It also leads away from any possible heritage. Believers in Christ have both: a firm, unmovable foundation and an eternal heritage with God forever. Atheists have neither. Unbelief in God is the single most undermining factor of one's security.

Agnosticism

Agnosticism is a system of unbelief that endeavors to remove the *risk* of a personal relationship with God. Agnostics tend to think of God as being an unknowable, unloving force. This false view does not demand nor invite an open, costly, risky relationship.

The enemy, agnosticism, hinders people from viewing their relationship with God as a personal relationship. If God is a Rock, but cannot be known by man, instability will continue to reign. The agnostic mind will cast God aside as though He was an unusable, valueless object.

Developing knowledge without relationships is a very common way to live. Agnosticism does the same. Relationships are considered to be too hazardous and costly. If someone makes a commitment to another, barriers are often removed. This opens people's lives up to the dangers of what others might do to them or think of them. They become vulnerable. Many people are treated with the cold calculating philosophy of agnosticism. Therefore, projecting their feelings toward God or toward anyone is considered by them to be a danger they do not want to face.

Deism is a common form of agnosticism. Deists believe that God created everything and then proceeded to turn away from His creation. They view God as powerful (Creator), but, uncaring. The teaching of deism leaves man no option of developing a personal relationship with God. To deists, God is perceived as one who is never present to help them.

The God of the Bible is not represented by agnosticism. The agnostic god is the product of man's inability to deal with life. Under agnosticism, all of life is considered to be the fateful work of an uncaring god or a force not worth knowing. In practice, the agnostic is no more secure than the atheist.

Gnosticism

Gnostics hold to a superior knowledge. They elevate their knowledge above the simplicity of the truths found in the Scriptures. Gnosticism brings much damage into the arena of God's intended purposes for man. Super knowledge or additional knowledge promoted as necessary to know God is very common, especially within cultic groups.

Other religions outside Christianity make claims of knowledge that are above Bible truths, equal to Bible truths, or separate from Bible truths. This "superior knowledge" may be religiously based. It may even be based upon isolated Bible truths or parts of Bible truths. However, gnosticism denies and rejects the simple argument that the Rock is *all* that man needs to be secure.

Common Gnostic statements may sound like this: "You can believe in Christ as your personal Savior if you want to, but you should also...". Or, "If you really want to know God, you need to see the Bible the way we do." Thus, the plain, yet profound biblical truths can be by-passed. A different rock becomes emphasized and substituted for the True Rock.

Gnosticism can be accepted by Christians under the guise of interpretation or spiritualization of the Scriptures. Observation of the simple truths of the Bible must never be compromised. The Bible says what it means and means what it says.

Our family built a house in Connecticut in the late 1950's. Many of the exterior walls were stone and stone veneer. As a child, I learned that there was a vast difference between a usable stone and sandstone. The usable stones were hard, like granite. Each one was tested with a blow from the hammer. The sandstones were unusable, soft and crumbly. One firm hammer blow would cause the stone to shatter into countless pieces of sand.

Gnosticism is like the sandstone. The Gnostic looks and sounds secure. But firm beatings from trials and tests reveal the insecurities of life. The Gnostic's beliefs eventually crumble into pieces of unusable opinions and philosophies.

Humanism

Humanism springs from the desires of mankind. It is a system of thought which has people as its center.

In this way, people place other weaker and temporary things in the place of the Eternal Rock. This is an anti (instead of) Christian point of view. Something or someone else has been substituted for the place that God has designed for Himself.

Humanism is the most common enemy that confronts the security of man. It puts on many faces, representing the many desires and whims of humanity. This popular viewpoint has built lofty structures of pride. Pride sounds like security, but it is not. Pride is built upon the weak foundation of the pseudo-goodness of man.

The proud and ultimately damning philosophies of personal independence and autonomy have been developed from humanism. When practiced, one observes a proud man standing alone with no foundation other than himself. The greatest difficulty with humanism is that it ignores the fact that people die. Where is the proud foundation of the humanist at the time of death? The legacy and heritage left by the humanist are mere pictures and shadows of security.

All four of the above mentioned enemies are related to one another; all four are systems of unbelief. Therefore, all four can be destroyed by faith in the Rock, the Lord Jesus Christ. It is no wonder why man resists knowing and receiving Jesus Christ by faith. *Receiving Christ would annihilate man's own present system of false security!*

Man's desire is to reason things out to the best of his understanding. Yet God has declared Himself to be known by man only through faith (Romans 10:17; Hebrews 11:6; John 3:16).

God's command and purpose brought forth to man is that of security: First Corinthians 15:58 says,

"Therefore, my beloved brethren, be steadfast, immovable, always abounding in the work of the Lord, knowing that your toil is not in vain in the Lord." The Bible commands people to be secure in the Lord. In all that God has commanded, He has also provided a way for man to achieve. This is also true regarding security. Since God has commanded believers to be steadfast and unmovable, there must be a way for them to obtain security.

Summary

Security is that feeling that we have when we know that all is well. This secure feeling is furthered when we believe and act according to the Truth. If we do not believe the Truth, we will not have the Truth (I John 5:1-12). If we do not have the Truth, we will not be able to live according to the Truth. If we do not live according to the Truth, we place ourselves into systems and theories that cause doubt. Doubt is not security. When we live in doubt, we live in insecurity. When we live in Truth, we live in confidence and safety.

We have two choices. On one hand, we can believe the Truth, possess the Truth, and live according to the Truth. This will grant us joy, fullness, confidence, and security.

On the other hand, we can reject the Truth. When Truth is rejected, another invented standard, system, or theory *must* replace it. These replacement standards are falsely imagined foundations which lead to systematic theories of doubt. Such theories of doubt and unbelief will lead only to fear, anxiety, and insecurity.

Chapter 2

<u>Security: Man's Basic Need</u>

"Needy, Needy," is the cry of man's empty heart self-willed,
As he walks this life, overrun with strife, with desires unfulfilled.
"Needy, Needy," man says, as from God He turns away,
Plotting his path, year after year, he's the same from day to day.

Security is that feeling one has when all is well. True secure feelings are entirely independent of circumstances. A storm may be raging on the outside, but the nursing baby is secure in his mother's bosom. Recall that *security is experienced when one knows all is well even when all is not well.* David wrote of this security he experienced in the Lord.

Psalm 34:4-7 -- "I sought the Lord, and He answered me, And delivered me from all my fears. They looked to Him and were radiant, And their faces shall never be ashamed. This poor man cried and the Lord heard him, And saved him out of all his troubles. The angel of the Lord encamps around those who fear Him, And rescues them."

15

Troubles abounded in David's life. The books of First and Second Samuel and Psalms testify of this. Yet, he had no troubles while he turned to the Lord and put his faith in Him. Note the word "all" in these above verses. Does this mean that all the trials *went away?* No! It means that David's confidence (faith) in the Lord removed fear and anxiety from his heart. Essentially, the absence of fear and anxiety is the absence of troubles. Manifesting faith in God, David was no longer troubled by his troubles.

Afflictions caused David to seek the Lord. In Psalm 119:71, David writes, "It is good for me that I was afflicted, That I may learn Thy statutes." As he sought the Lord, he realized that life was not about trials. He realized that life was about his relationship to God.

The same trusting characteristics should be in the life of every believer today. Trials and tests are everywhere. However, the trusting Christian is safe and secure in the arms of the Lord. Does this mean that believers experience no discomforts? Not at all! Discomforts cannot take away the security given by the Lord. Nor can comforts cause a person to become more secure in the Lord.

It may be that some people have never grown up. As children, if they could not get a certain toy or piece of candy, they felt their parents were angry with them. As adults, they may have the same insecure feelings toward God. If God does not allow them to have certain comforts and possessions, they may feel that God is angry with them. Security for children is based upon having right relationships with parents, not upon candy and toys. Security for adults is based on having right relationships with God, not upon comforts and possessions.

We need to realize this as we journey through life. Life is not about comfort. Nor, is it about tribulations. *Life is about God.* When this principle is incorporated into our lives, we will see life from God's point of view.

Death: Insecurity Expressed

God's intention for Adam and Eve was to have them living safe, secure lives upon the earth. When the trespass occurred in the Garden of Eden (Genesis 3), the whole human race was plunged into insecurity. Mankind's relationship to God was demolished. In one act of disobedience, all people became separated from God (Romans 5:12). Separation from God is entirely opposite to the sense of belonging to family and community.

There can be no greater expression of insecurity than death. Death is the weakness which expresses the ultimate of all human frailties.

People have searched for the Holy Grail. They have invented and tried to find the fountain of youth. Multitudes try to cover up the aging process. Wigs, facial creams, make-up, and cosmetic surgery are commonplace. Even while standing before a casket, people will remark as they regard the corpse, "My, he looks pretty good, doesn't he?", or "Isn't there a great expression of peace on his face?"

With strides in medicine, man has taken credit for increasing the average life expectancy of people. Sparing no expense or effort, man has decided to prolong his life as long as he possibly can. Operations involving transplants and transfusions are very common. The intended purpose is so that one might physically live longer and better.

Medicine has also tried to deal with the problem by providing tranquilizers for all those who are in need of security. This is done so that insecure people will be "tranquil." From toddler to old age, there are drugs to bring people up and drugs to bring people down. Man feels that it has become extremely important not to face insecurities of any kind. Pills are available for almost any need cited by man.

Some have even gone so far as to have their dead bodies frozen with the intent of being revived at some future date. Even if their dead bodies could be given new life, they would still have to face the insecurities of life and death in their future.

Ignoring or denying insecurity will not make us secure. Boasting about and claiming security does not cause security. These are merely mankind's ways of denying the weaknesses of our lives. When our weakness to cope with life and death is denied, we can become like ostriches, burying our heads in the sand.

When we were children we may have claimed safety as we pulled the bed covers over our heads during a nighttime thunderstorm. We close our eyes while riding tall roller coasters. If we fall from the top story of the Empire State Building, the result will be death. Closing our eyes will not stop the process of falling. We are all falling, falling... .

Death is our enemy. We can dress it up. We can ignore it. We can tell others that death does not exist from out of our imaginative inventions. The belief in reincarnation is another weak attempt to hide from the inevitable consequence of sin. That inevitable consequence is death! We can try to ease the pain of death with drugs. We can try to do away with the anxiety of it. None of these things work. Death still comes. It is harsh. It is real. It is impartial. There are those who are fed up with life because of their insecurities. They want to end their lives. They do not believe that life will improve. So they take an active part to end their lives themselves. The driving need for the desired elusive security becomes so strong that suicide seems to be their only answer. Strange as it may seem, death is preferred instead of the necessary answer: genuine faith and trust in God.

The Appearance and Value of Security

Psychologists and psychiatrists have spent countless hours striving to help their clients become more secure in living life. They have gone to great measures to explore deep down into the souls (psyches) of their patients. They agonize, sympathize, and empathize with them in their struggle for security. Yet, where do therapists go to find the security that they themselves need? Where is *their* foundation? Where is *their* "rock?"

Society recognizes the value of security. Those who claim insecurity by the fault of others may be awarded large sums of money by the judicial system. If physical or emotional trauma is introduced into a person's life by an offending party, the offending party becomes liable. Great dollar amounts have been received by those suffering anxiety caused by some careless person.

Work-out programs and gymnasiums continue to increase. People are looking for the perfect abdominal muscles. The message given is that people must improve their health for the future. Diet gurus and diet drugs have exploded into a multi-billion dollar industry. All this, and more is done so that people can claim security and really look as if they have security.

When I was twelve years old, my grandmother gave me a pair of ice skates for Christmas. I couldn't wait to use them. This particular winter in the northern portion of Connecticut was fairly mild, but cold enough to freeze the lakes and ponds. I was convinced that all was well. The ground was frozen even though there was no snow on the ground. Lake Ayapo looked especially inviting, smooth as glass. I strapped on the skates. I sailed out onto the lake, the wind whistling by my ears. Faster, faster I skated! What fun! Then, the fall. Wham! A small hole (two inches in diameter) appeared where I had landed. Cracks developed in every direction! I was *very* insecure! I picked myself up and gingerly made my way back to shore and back to security.

In the lives of many, the *look* of security has replaced the truth of security. Lake Ayapo looked safe enough for ice skating. In truth, it was not.

"Success": Man's Attempt for Security

Job security is sought after in the work force. Employees seek and scheme for promotions with such effort that ethical means are often discarded.

Insurance and investment industries have prospered greatly. The concept promoted is to "help" people obtain financial security and independence. This trend continues.

I viewed a presentation by an investment firm recently. The approach was interesting, yet typical. Money was presented as being equal to freedom. Yet, it was stated that their goal was not money, but rather, the things money buys (a little double talk). Security was defined by "being able to provide for the future." People were told to dream and to follow their dreams. The most subtle part of the presentation included the family. It was stated that the goal was to "create wealth for families." I surmised that this last statement was designed to take away the guilt caused by promoting the sin of covetousness.

A long list of expected successful appearances from the world is constantly being placed before people: clothes with a particular label, automobiles with specific engines, boats with greater horsepower, houses in a particular neighborhood, etc. All these things and more may give the appearance of security without providing the real thing.

Children long to know that their parents love them. They yearn to experience the care that rightly belongs to them. Throughout the development of a child's life, times of insecurity arise due to various events. These events may be the death of one or both parents, the separation or divorce of the parents, uncaring or unkind parents, broken promises, accidents of varying severity, illnesses and diseases, and cruelty from outside the home. Parents, teachers, coaches, and peers may place undue pressure upon the lives of children.

An endless list of frustrations may be named as the cause of insecurity. All children will face the dangers of insecurity as they develop into adults. It is inevitable.

The need for security is so strong that young children will go to great lengths to grasp for it. They will suffer abuse and still show a desire to please their parents. They will obey parents without question or complaint. When a child reaches adolescence and security is still absent, rebellion often occurs. Improper sexual activity, substance abuse, and gang involvement may be spawned from a desire to be accepted by peers. The driving need to be accepted into a family of peers can become the single focus of a person's life.

The above mentioned activities are often responses to the absence of security. The need for the feeling of community, family, belonging to something or someone *must* be met. When it is not provided in a good and acceptable manner, it will be sought after and obtained in any way possible. Only later do people realize that they have merely jumped from one lonely path of expectant hope to another.

Many marriages have been entered into with the wrong expectancy. One or both of the spouses may endeavor to find their self-worth in one another. They may feel that if they could only have a particular person as husband or wife, they would be happy and secure for life. All of their unfulfilled needs are planned to be siphoned out of this new relationship of love and stability. When this does not take place, the result is the same as the beginning, before the relationship was established. In fact, their insecurities may be deepened by the experiences of disappointment and distrust.

When the basic needs of security are not met, marriage partners can be driven to fulfill those needs anywhere they can. Men and women become workaholics. New friendships and new sexual relationships will often occur. Either one or both parties may enter into the so-called "mid-life crisis." Alcohol, substance abuse, or even legal drugs may enter into adults' lives due to the pressures of these insecurities.

Education, the development of the mind and the thinking processes, and the attainments of certain academic goals are noteworthy and noble endeavors. However, this too can be an empty water hole of misplaced trust. One must remember that the thinking of *all* the former minds on earth has ended. The greatest philosophers, scientists, and engineers of the past have never been able to stop their own deterioration and weaknesses. The insecure process of death knows no academic boundaries. No one is exempt. There are no supermen in the world.

The arts and the appreciation of them are also mere bandages. They cover and soothe only the outside of the putrefying sores caused by the sinfulness of man. When the music stops, the only sound is the lonely heart of despair, anxiety, and desperation. Life is seen for what it really is. It is not a symphony. To the person lacking security, life is a jumble of discordant notes with no meaning or purpose.

Summary

Man cannot escape from the truth of his basic need for security. Without food he would starve to death. Similarly, without security he will not be able to function in the freedom that God has promised. Before man's fall in the garden of Eden, he freely spoke to God, and God to him. After the fall of Adam & Eve, an entirely different picture is seen (Genesis 3:8). God is seen walking in the cool of the day in the garden, looking for the same relationship that He and His creation formerly enjoyed. Instead, He found two frightened, irresponsible, and insecure people.

Security is the basic need of people everywhere. Some have found security in God through the Lord Jesus Christ. Others have thought they had found it elsewhere, only to be disappointed at a later time. Many people may feel secure because they deny that they are insecure.

Many claim security by appearing secure. There are many who keep searching for something that will make them secure.

Chapter 3

Eternity: Last Things First

Forever Secure in eternity, Oh what steadfast hope and joy!
To know that God will keep His Word, our faith he'll not destroy.
For as we travel through life's journey, knowing that God is true,
We sing as we go, on this road below, to give God His praises due.

Although it may sound odd to begin at the end, it is the right thing to do. If life is looked upon as a journey, one needs to have his destination clearly in mind. When one goes on a trip, he first determines where he is going. He finds the location on a map and then decides how to get there.

Regarding life, the end of man's journey is eternity. If one knows that he is going to make it to the end of his journey (eternity with God), the rest of the journey will not seem quite so difficult. The journey is temporary. The end is permanent. Unfortunately, many get caught up in the journey. They do not realize the priceless value of their destination.

Most people can live their entire lives with no assurance that the end of their journey is securely in place. Doubt, fear, anxiety, and insecurity will be manifested throughout such a trip. As a result, all the traveling done to arrive there will certainly be filled with the emptiness of vanity. King Solomon wrote in Ecclesiastes 1:2 -- "Vanity of vanities," says the Preacher, "Vanity of vanities! All is vanity."

God has given us His Word in which He declares that His purpose for the believer is to know his destination. The believer is to know that he has eternal life. "These things I have written to you who believe in the name of the Son of God, in order that you may know that you have eternal life." (I John 5:13). Eternal life is the end of the journey that God has freely offered to man. If a person has eternal life and knows that he has it, then the end of life is already looked upon as being successful. What greater confidence and joy can there be in one's life than this? The peace and joy caused by this knowledge will result in a life of confidence.

In this chapter, the topic of eternal security will be dealt with from two major points: from the nature of God and from the nature of man.

1) The Nature of God

Titus 1:1,2 -- "Paul, a bond-servant of God, and an apostle of Jesus Christ, for the faith of those chosen of God and the knowledge of the truth which is according to godliness, in the hope of eternal life, which God, who cannot lie, promised long ages ago."

The nature of God is one of complete honesty and integrity. The characteristics of mankind do not include complete honesty and integrity. When God is described by the attributes of man rather than His own, His integrity will soon be questioned.

A young man spoke to me about salvation and asked, "How can I know that God is telling the truth?" Such a question is filled with a lack of knowledge and faith concerning the character of God. I used the above verses to show him that it is not possible for God to lie. When God has said that He has given eternal life to all believers in Christ, He is telling the truth.

John 10:27-29 -- "My sheep hear My voice, and I know them, and they follow Me; and I give eternal life to them, and they shall never perish; and no one shall snatch them out of My hand. My Father, who has given them to Me, is greater than all; and no one is able to snatch them out of the Father's hand."

Eternal life is eternal. It lasts forever. If this eternal life that God has promised and given to His people ceases, it is not eternal. If it is taken away, it is not eternal. It then becomes temporary life. If God meant temporary life, He would have said "temporary life." The permanent characteristic of this life is again established in these verses by "and they shall never perish." Just in case one does not understand eternal life, God has given His inspired commentary in verse 28. There is no mistake as to what God is saying. This inspired commentary (the Bible) defines eternal life: "never perish."

If God is not being honest in this one area (or any other area of Scripture), then His whole plan and all His Word are to be questioned. Many people believe that the Bible teaches that people must receive Christ as their personal Savior. They believe that their sins are washed away by the sacrifice that Christ made on the cross for them. However, some of these same people deny that the new life given to them is eternal. This is a blatant denial of the teaching of the Word of God.

How do such people know that *any* of their sins are forgiven? If God has lied about the eternal part of this salvation, how can they be remotely sure He is telling the truth about forgiveness? The answer is: they cannot be sure. They must always live in doubt of even the simple truth of forgiveness. They must doubt all other biblical truths. After all, the same God spoke each one of the truths in the Bible.

The veracity and omnipotence of God are great truths. In John 10:28, He says that no one *will* take the believer in Christ away from Him. This means that it is not going to happen. The integrity of God and His Word are at stake here.

Furthermore, in John 10:29, Jesus informs us that no one has the capability to accomplish such a deed as to take the believer from the hand of God. God's power is at stake here. There are only two ways that a believer can lose his salvation: 1) His salvation must be confronted by a force more powerful than the omnipotent God, or 2) The believer himself must become more powerful than God. Obviously, neither of these things can happen. The only way these truths can be denied is simply not to believe them.

God's nature in His dealings with believers and unbelievers has always been that of grace. Romans 3:24 says, "being justified as a gift by His grace through the redemption which is in Christ Jesus." God's grace has always been defined as "unmerited favor," getting something that has not been earned, nor deserved. Even those who do not believe in eternal security hold to this definition. This salvation is a gift. A gift is different from a loan. There are requirements and conditions placed upon a loan; it must be paid back to the creditor in full. However, a gift is freely given, without requirements or conditions.

Ephesians 2:8,9 -- "For by grace you have been saved through faith; and that not of yourselves, it is the gift of God; not as a result of works, that no one should boast."

If the gift of eternal life (Romans 6:23 -- "the gift of God is eternal life") given by God is considered to be loan, it is not a gift. If God takes away this gift, then it was never intended to be a gift. This brings us back to the former discussion regarding the integrity of God. Those who accuse God of taking eternal life away from believers accuse God of saying "gift" when He really meant to say, "loan."

Faith and Perfection

Why has God accepted the faith of the believer as a means of granting justification, rather than a person's works (Romans 3:28; 5:1)? God has declared the believing sinner righteous. This declaration is made on the basis of the righteousness of Jesus Christ, not on the basis of man's deeds and sacrifices. II Corinthians 5:21 says, "He made Him who knew no sin to be sin on our behalf, that we might become the righteousness of God in Him."

God is perfect and demands perfection from all people. Matthew 5:48 says, "Be ye therefore perfect, even as your Father which is in heaven is perfect." There is a way to satisfy the perfect, righteous character of God. One must be seen by God as just as righteous as God Himself. The only way that this can be accomplished is by faith in the Lord Jesus Christ, the

Righteous One. Then, God makes His declaration of Christ's righteousness upon the believing sinner.

2) The Nature of Man

The nature of man is that of weakness; he is by act and definition incomplete. Romans 8:3 tells us that the law of God was only weak because it could not be performed by man: "For what the Law could not do, weak as it was *through the flesh*, God did: sending His own Son in the likeness of sinful flesh and as an offering for sin, He condemned sin in the flesh." (italics -- mine). God's standard (perfection -- Matthew 5:48) could not be met by weak, sinful, fleshly man.

As one would evaluate the works of man, which works would be good enough for a perfect God? Would not the Perfect Righteous Judge be offended at the puny, insignificant attempts of mankind to obtain His approval through their imperfect tainted works? Yes, He would be offended, and indeed He is!

Pharmaceutical companies measure their medicines in milligrams. When a person ingests a tablet of 100 mg, how does he know it is 100 mg? How does the manufacturer know that it is 100 mg? The answer is: they measured it. But, is it perfectly 100 mg? Is it possible that it could be 100.000000000000001 mg? Or perhaps, one of the pills is 99.99999999999999999 mg. It is not only possible, but absolutely certain. Is that perfection? No!

Shakespeare's play, "The Merchant of Venice," is an intriguing drama. Portia defended her client aptly when she demanded that Shylock fulfill the law perfectly. She demanded that Shylock take only a pound of flesh from his unfortunate quarry. Shylock was to take no more nor no less than a pound of flesh.

The contract did not allow him to take any blood. It did not allow him to take life away from his victim. Because Portia demanded perfection, the contract became invalid.

It is obvious! Man cannot attain to his own self-decreed "perfect" standards. How can anyone possibly be fooled into thinking that God's standards are less than or even equal to man's? God is the only One who is perfect. His standards cannot be satisfied by the imperfect attempts of mankind.

If people think that they will cause themselves to be saved or keep themselves saved by their imperfect efforts, they are wrong. They will be saved only by the perfect sacrifice of the Son of God for their sins. They will be kept only by that same sacrifice that saved them. The work of Christ is completely acceptable to God to save *and* to keep the believer forever.

Neither the works of the believer nor the works of the unbeliever add to the completeness of Christ's sacrifice. Adding to the perfect work of Christ (gnosticism) sends an offensive message to God. It tells Him that the death of His Son was not complete enough nor perfect enough for man.

Romans 3:23 "...for all have sinned and fall short of the glory of God," vividly points out another insurmountable problem with which man is faced. He is a sinner. He is offensive to God. He is spiritually dead (Ephesians 2:1).

Eternal security has been questioned by many on the basis of qualifying sins into categories. These categories include sins and "serious sins." They feel that they are saved because of what Jesus Christ has done for them. He died for them, forgave them, and gave them a new life. But, if they sin "too much" or commit some "serious sin," then they no longer feel saved.

One may point out here that such people may not be trusting Christ for their salvation. It is possible that they have always been trusting in their own ability to stay away from "serious sin." Thus, they have been entrusting their salvation to their own merit and abilities rather than to the grace of God.

I spoke with a woman regarding this matter of eternal security. She had previously professed Christ as her Savior and had manifested many good Christian qualities. However, there were still doubts in her mind regarding the security of her eternal destiny in heaven. Together, we went through God's plan of salvation a second time. She obtained the needed victory after asking Christ to be her Savior again. I asked what it was that made the difference. She replied, "Previously, I did not view myself as a 'really bad' person. I had never sinned the sin of adultery." She was now confident that she was eternally secure. Now, she was trusting Christ rather than her own "good" desire to stay away from sinning a "serious sin."

The nature of sin before God does not allow us to hold to the "serious sin" view. James 2:10-11 tells us:

"For whoever keeps the whole law and yet stumbles in one point, he has become guilty of all. For He who said, 'Do not commit adultery,' also said, 'Do not commit murder.' Now if you do not commit adultery, but do commit murder, you have become a transgressor of the law."

In addition, Jesus taught in Matthew 5:21,22 and 5:27,28 that sin is not merely an outward matter (transgression). Hatred and lust (iniquities) in the sight of God are just as sinful as murder and adultery. *All sin is serious!*

At times, professing Christians cite the presence of an "unpardonable" sin or a "mortal" sin as a means of losing the free gift of eternal life. The context of Matthew 12:31 does not support this teaching. The following reasons will help one find a proper understanding of Jesus' teachings in Matthew 12.

First, Jesus was speaking of a special event in history. Christ's teachings in Matthew 12 were in response to the refusal of the Pharisees to accept His work as authentic (from God). Nowhere else in Scripture does one find this event repeated. If this event was the normal approach to the doctrine of salvation, there would be other supportive events with the same condemnation brought forth from the Lord.

Second, the Pharisees had accused Christ of casting out demons by using demonic powers. This accusation equated Christ with Satan. One who believes that Christ and Satan are the same person is certainly not a believer in the biblical Christ.

This blasphemy against the ministry of the Holy Spirit is based upon what a person believes about Christ. Jesus was talking about the requirements for salvation. The Pharisees were denying the deity of the Lord Jesus Christ as represented to them by the Holy Spirit of God. This is the particular sin which was being addressed by Christ in this context.

There are doctrines concerning Christ that must be believed in order for one to be a Christian. Anyone who does not believe these teachings is not a child of God. The specifics of one's necessary faith are plainly revealed to us in Romans 10:9,10. One specific requirement is to believe that Jesus Christ is God:

"that if you confess with your mouth Jesus as Lord, and believe in your heart that God raised Him from the dead, you shall be saved; for with the heart man believes, resulting in righteousness, and with the mouth he confesses, resulting in salvation."

The Pharisees were denying these necessary teachings. They were not professing "Jesus as Lord." They were professing "Jesus as Satan." While they held such a view of Christ, it was not possible for forgiveness to be a part of their lives.

The question to be posed before the erroneous "serious sin" view is, "How big of a sin must you commit before God does not allow you to go to heaven?" When this question was asked a teenage boy, he answered, "If I deny Christ and turn away from Him, He will not allow me into heaven." A total misunderstanding of the nature of sin in God's sight is represented by this answer. Others who have this view may answer, "If I become a child abuser or rapist," or, "If I never attend church services again," or, "If I break my vows before God and cheat on my spouse." All these answers are born from the lack of knowing the seriousness of *all* sin. All people everywhere stand as sinners before a Holy, Sinless, Perfect God.

The error of "sinless perfection" comes from the teaching of eternal insecurity. Those who hold this view may testify that they have not sinned for "thirty-six years." What they mean is that they have not sinned like they used to sin; or they have not sinned one of the big "serious sins." This false view may give them a sense of protection. They must say, "We have not sinned." Otherwise, they cannot fool themselves into thinking they are heaven bound. However, false statements and beliefs will not cause security, joy, and peace.

Denial of sin never leads to forgiveness and salvation. First John 1:8-10 tells us that the denial of sin is a lie. Confession that one is a sinner before God leads to forgiveness, cleansing, and eternal salvation.

Summary

The first thing for all people to take care of is the last thing: eternity. Without eternity taken care of, life loses purpose and direction. If the final destination of man is obscured by the clouds of doubt and fear, then much anxiety results during the journey toward that destination.

Questions arise along the way: "Does God really love me enough to save me forever? Am I acceptable to God? How can I prove myself to be worthy of God today? Since I am unsure of God's eternal love, how can I be sure His love is upon me today?" Such questions will cause people to change their paths over and over again. With these questions and doubts, they will never be sure they are on the right road.

Personal Reflection

I ask you, dear reader, to pause and to reflect on these biblical truths. Have you personally received Christ's sacrifice for your sins to be sufficient for you? Have you by faith simply bowed before the Lord to confess that you are a guilty condemned sinner? If you have never done so, I encourage you to ask Christ to save you by faith, believing that His violent bloody death was for your sins.

Chapter 4

Experiencing Security With Christ

The World is filled with doubt and fear, and our eyesight may grow dim,
With guessing gone we take God's Word, and trust completely in Him.
He takes our hands, upheld by trust, and puts them to labor on earth,
By His will, He assures our hearts, that we're His children by new birth.

How do we know that we know? Is this a guess, a leap into the dark? A leap into the dark certainly does not sound like security. People have many doubts and fears regarding whether or not they really know the Lord Jesus Christ. However, we really can know!

There are two main Greek words used in the New Testament for our English word "know." One is pronounced "ginosko," which means to know by experience. The other is pronounced "oida," which means to know intrinsically, without going through a learning experience.

First John 5:13 tells us that the Word of God was written so that believers would know (oida -- to know intrinsically) that they have eternal life. This is not something that they have to experience before they know they have it. If one waits to experience eternity before they receive the free gift of eternal life, it will be too late.

This is the common philosophy in our society: *"Let me feel it first, then I will make a choice on the basis of my experience."* Today, everything is tried on for size before a commitment is made. This is true whether it is a marriage or a pair of blue jeans. It is not possible to receive eternal life on a trial basis. Eternal life is entered into on the basis of receiving the Son of God by faith (I John 5:10-12), not by some experience.

First John 3:24 uses the other word for know, "ginosko." How does the believer know by experience that Jesus Christ is remaining in him? The Holy Spirit gives this knowledge only as the Christian practices obedience to Christ (keeps His commandments).

A believer who is not obeying the Lord is going to have much insecurity. He will not experience the abiding presence of Jesus Christ. Eternal life is not in jeopardy here. The intrinsic knowledge of eternal salvation is a part of the believer forever. However, in his daily living, it is possible for the Christian to experience insecurity. Insecurity is experienced because of disobedience on his part.

Jesus taught that believers are to be obedient. John 15 teaches that obedient believers have the abiding, fellowshipping, remaining presence of Christ.

Disobedient believers are not abiding in Christ. The Bible speaks of serious consequences for the disobedient Christian, even physical illness and death (I Corinthians 11:30; I John 5:16; John 15:6). Once again, eternal salvation is not the topic being addressed in these verses. The words of John 15 by the Lord are words demanding obedience. A person is never placed into God's family by acts of obedience. It is well established that this eternal life can be entered into

37

only by faith (Ephesians 2:8,9). Thus, John 15 must be speaking of fellowship caused by obedience. Conversely, it is talking about a lack of fellowship caused by disobedience.

Secure relationships of love and unity are established in the lives of people as they dwell together. This is called "abiding." Family members living in the same house can develop secure relationships. Husbands, wives, grown children, mothers, fathers, and grandparents all come and go without question. The practice of responsibility, respect, kindness, love, mercy, and graciousness contributes to a secure family atmosphere. Such family members are viewed as reliable. People living in this kind of home appreciate each other based upon the experiences they have previously established with one another.

This is also true when the believer makes the words of Christ a living reality in his practice. A close, trusting, secure fellowship with the Son of God is experienced.

When one or more of the members of a household are continuously breaking the family rules, negative consequences are experienced. Family members are then viewed as unreliable (insecure). Much confusion and instability will govern the atmosphere of that home. Yet, each one remains a member of that particular family.

This is also true in the believer's relationship with the Lord Jesus Christ. When a Christian disobeys, he remains in God's family, but lives in confusion and doubt.

Christ and the believer are to grow closer and closer together. This is accomplished as the believer faithfully adheres to the commands of Christ (the rules that Christ has for *His* family). However, when those commands are broken, confusion and instability will rule God's spiritual family. Jesus said in John 15:11, "These things I have spoken to you, that My joy may be in you, and that your joy may be made full." Following Christ is meant to be a life of joyful security, not a life of doubt and unhappiness.

Some look upon the commandments of Christ as being restrictive and burdensome. *This view will cause a lack of fellowship with Christ. Lack of fellowship with Christ will not promote freedom in the life of the Christian.* Jesus taught clearly that believers, continuing in His truth and following His commands, live in great freedom. The obedient believer is set free from the bondage caused by all other things.

Unredeemed man and the carnal Christian always look at God's commandments as confining (Psalm 2:2 -- "Let us tear their fetters apart, And cast away their cords from us!"). God laughs at the folly that man brings upon himself (Psalm 2:4 -- "He who sits in the heavens laughs, The Lord scoffs at them"). By setting himself free from God's laws, man becomes a slave to his own inferior ideas, ambitions, doubts, and sins.

Summary

In Philippians 3:10, Paul spoke of his desire to know Christ by experience. The word for "know" used here is "ginosko." It is obvious that the Apostle Paul is not talking about a desire to become a Christian. He was expressing his desire to have a full Christian experience in his life. A full Christian experience is equal to the sweet success of obedience and fellowship. Experiential knowledge gained by obedience results in peaceful security.

The only way a person can know the security that the Lord gives is to submit to the plan that God has outlined in His Word. Without obedience, the believer does not lose his salvation, but he does *not* experience security. With obedience, the Christian knows that he is experiencing Christ. It ought to be the longing desire of every believer to experience the Lord Jesus Christ in his daily walk. The confidence which God gives to obedient Christians will characterize their lives with peace and joy.

Chapter 5

Our Sovereign God

With wisdom God rules, He puts the king in his place.
His knowledge never falters as He brings forth His grace.
Righteousness encompasses all that He does every day.
Honor, integrity, veracity, and truth all light His way.

One of the greatest masqueraders of security is human control or domination. When a person is in control of someone or something, he may experience a false sense of security. Yet, the desire to be in control may very well have sprung from insecurity. One might reason it this way: "If I am in control, then the results will be what I would like them to be. People have failed me time after time. I am not going to allow them to fail me again. If I want the job done right, I will have to do it myself. I will have to control others so that they will not embarrass me."

Insecurity is one of the bases for the need to be domineering. The following are brief illustrations relating insecurity to domination: If I am married, I will do everything possible to get *my* spouse to conform to *my* values and to *my* way of thinking. If I am a parent, I will dominate every decision and activity of *my* child. If I am a child, I will do *my* best to control *my* parents and other authorities to do *my*

41

bidding. If I am a pastor of a church, I will not give *my* church members the freedom to make responsible decisions. If I am a manager, I will hover over *my* workers until they are in complete submission to *my* ways.

The pressure to be in control knows no age limit. I remember my children bantering with one another over candy. The comment was, "If you don't give me a piece of candy, I won't be your friend." This did not always work. Sometimes, the response would be, "Okay, I don't need you as my friend. You can't have any of my candy!" It was then time to teach a lesson on sharing. However, I was still glad that my children could not be pressured into some kind of action based upon their need for "friendship."

Insecure adults also use these pressures as a ploy to gain an upper hand over others. The piece of candy that the child used is merely discarded for another form of enticement. The enticement could be in the form of peer pressure, money, a nice home-cooked dinner, sexual advances, or even kind words and deeds. The result is still the same "candy friendship" which some children have.

Insecurities are all symptoms of a bigger problem that we have. The larger problem is that we do not believe that *God* is in control of all things. We may have erroneously learned that He needs our help.

Genesis records the account of Abraham and Sarah. God had promised a son to Abraham. Abraham waited and waited. No son was born to him through Sarah. Sarah came up with the idea that maybe God needed their help. She convinced Abraham to take her slave, Hagar, as his concubine. Hagar conceived and bore a son, Ishmael. Ishmael was not the son that God had promised to Abraham. He was a son born out of fleshly motives. God later gave Abraham and Sarah the son of promise, Isaac. God did not need their help. They merely needed to believe that God was in control.

Believing that God is in control will give the believer great peace, confidence, and security. One does not have to connive or step outside ethical means in order to "work things out."

Two responsibilities are put into practice by the Christian who is trusting in God as the Sovereign God: working for God and waiting on God. Trusting God has never been synonymous with laziness. *If one believes God, he will want to follow a plan of activity that is pleasing to God.* Nor is trusting God characterized by a life of worry. Worry and trust are opposites. Trust is the basis for the activity of waiting upon the Lord.

A more subtle way of dismissing the sovereignty of God is to say: "We need His help." This is a true statement. We truly *do* need God's help! We are in *constant* need of God's help. However, what one might mean is that we do not need God's help until we have exhausted all of *our* resources of strength and ingenuity.

I was attending a meeting at which a Christian college was being represented by the testimonies of some of its students. One student said, "I have learned to do all that I can. Then, when I can do no more, I trust the Lord to do the rest." This is an unfortunate, yet very common view among Christians.

What happened to the Scriptural teachings that the Lord is to be completely involved in *all* that we do (I Corinthians 10:31)? What happened to God being looked upon as Sovereign of the universe? Does He not care about everything? If He needs us to control things, then He must not be in control. Is God constantly giving us control of things and then taking that control away from us? A god who operates in this fashion is certainly not the God of the Bible.

Most people have comparative joy. I was visiting one of my elderly church members in the hospital. She was facing gall bladder surgery. I tried to encourage her with Godly concern and some Bible verses. My desire as her pastor was to see her have the joy of trusting the Lord. Her response was this: "I praise the Lord, because I know I could be much worse physically than I am now. There are many people that have greater physical problems than I have."

This view of comparative joy is commonplace, but also, misguided. Finding joy for myself because others are less fortunate than me is a terrible concept.

Comparative joy is not joy based upon Bible truth. If I find joy in being better off than someone else, the opposite is also true. There will always be those who are better off than I am. Not only will I compare myself to the poor and needy, but also to the rich and famous. This comparative joy robs people of knowing that God's will is always best for them. He makes no mistakes. He is sovereign and His plan for us is the best. Let us rejoice in God's will rather than in our circumstances.

What I wanted to hear my elderly hospitalized church member say was this: "God is in control of all things. I have great joy in my heart that I know Him. No matter what the outcome of this surgery, I know that He loves me and that His plan is perfect for me."

Prayer pressure is also used as a means to obtain the intended result of a particular event. Nowhere do we find in Scripture that God is pressured into keeping the rain off our church picnics if we pray about it. Yet, we enlist thousands of people across the country to pray for the "success" of an event. This event may be an evangelistic crusade, a missionary hostage crisis, or a miraculous healing.

Usurping the authority of the Lord will never guarantee the outcome of any problem that we face. Yet, it is practiced by insecure people everywhere. Even if we "pray about it," God is still the One Who is in control of all things. Yes, we ought to pray. However, the will of our Sovereign God is to be our desire in all of our prayers, not our wills.

People with controlling lifestyles not only push away the authority of the Lord, but earthly authorities as well. Romans 13:1 says, "Let every person be in subjection to the governing authorities. For there is no authority except from God, and those which exist are established by God." Stepping outside these earthly authorities is equal to rebelling against God. Elected and appointed officials, husbands, parents, teachers, and church officers are authorities ordained by God. If God is looked upon as not being in control, then all authorities appointed by Him cannot be trusted. Fear and distrust rule the lives of all who do not view God as sovereign.

If God is perceived as not being sovereign, then He must not be in control. He is then accused by man of making mistakes. If God is making mistakes, then man must take control of every situation that he can. He must get everything to work out to the best of his ability.

Matthew 6 has much to say about trusting the Sovereign God for daily, practical sustenance.

Everyone's health, wealth, perceived beauty, length of life, food, clothing, and shelter are in the hands of God. Matthew 6 does not excuse people from working diligently. Neither is mankind exempt from making wise decisions with their finances, or lack thereof. However, this passage of Scripture teaches that God is to be trusted for the outcome of all man's labors and struggles.

Man is not in control of anything. God is in control of everything. Yet, it is easier for some people to try to make themselves taller than to simply trust the Lord to use them as short people.

In Matthew 6:19-34 the following three major principles of trusting God as sovereign are taught:

1) The place of our treasure reveals the place of our trust. Earthly possessions, earthly knowledge, earthly fame, and earthly abilities can all be erroneously trusted. However, God is sovereign over all. Things will never make us secure. They are all so temporary. Since security is not caused by possessions, the opposite is also true. The absence of things can never make us insecure. The place of our trust is what is all important.

When our trust is in the Sovereign God, peace and security are experienced. Worry is a sin because it is based upon a lack of trust in God. God is both great and good. If He is in control, we have no need to worry. *If He is not in control, we have every reason to worry!*

I own two automobiles. One is a 1993 economy car. The other is an old 1978 "junker." I have always driven old cars and economy-type vehicles. Recently, I was given a ride in one of the more expensive luxury cars. It was an awesome automobile! Not only did it have power everything, but everything had power! The car practically glided down the highway. However, as I viewed the interior and the exterior of this expensive piece of machinery, I made an observation. This luxury automobile was made from the same materials as my inexpensive cars: metal, plastic, rubber, and glass. The point is: I was just as secure in my "cheap" cars as I was in the luxury car. They were both temporary, physical items.

2) Life must be scrutinized with the singularity of the sovereignty of God in mind. The double vision of Matthew 6 could be interpreted as: one moment viewing life as though God was in control of all things, the next as though we are in control of some things. Such activity by the believer will lead to an unhealthy spiritual outlook. Singularity of vision will keep us focused on one thing -- the Gracious God who has all of life in His hands.

3) Since God is in sovereign control of all things, He is to be sought after with great diligence. Seeking the good of *His* realm and *His* rule is more important than seeking the things under His realm. This is defined for us in Matthew 6: 33. We do this by seeking *His* Righteousness. His righteousness is found in the person of His Son. Jesus Christ alone is God's righteousness for the believer.

Trusting in the Sovereign God and seeking the Sovereign God are primary essentials for true biblical security. Since God is in sovereign control of all things, faith in Him is not an option. Bad things happen when faith is placed in people, possessions, or circumstances. Confusion, worry, and disappointment will govern one's attitude. Believing that God is truly the Almighty God will revitalize a person's outlook in all things.

Sovereignty and Responsibility

God has given us hands with which to work and minds with which to think. His intended purpose is that we place all that we are and all that we have under His sovereign love and grace. We are in control of nothing. We are to manifest self-control. Yet, even self-control is caused by the Word of God controlling us through the ministry of the Holy Spirit (Galatians 5:22,23). It is the peaceful work of God in our hearts as we trust the Sovereign God Who is in control.

God is Sovereign. He rules and reigns over all things. He manifests His own free will as it pleases Him. He does what He wants to do without any fear that His plans will fail.

Some object to the idea that God is the sovereign Ruler, controlling all things. The argument employed is that a Sovereign God cannot hold man responsible for his actions. This argument is flawed. Man's responsibility under the Sovereign God does not diminish, but rather, is heightened. God in His sovereignty has planned to use man to perform His will. Strange as it seems, God has planned to work through people to accomplish His bidding.

Therefore, under God's sovereign rule, man's actions are accentuated. The trusting Christian knows that the performances of his responsibilities are directly fulfilling the plan of God. This is exciting! Believing in the sovereignty of God provides direction and purpose. Without the truth of God's sovereignty, man is in a constant guessing game of doubt and fear. No wonder there are so many nervous, unfulfilled, unhappy people in the world!

A great earthly king is called the sovereign of his

kingdom. He is responsible for his kingdom. Having full authority over his entire kingdom, he sets goals that will enhance his rule. In the process of fulfilling those goals, he requires various responsibilities to be performed by his subjects. He even goes so far as to force people to obey him. This scenario has been repeated time after time upon this earth. No one dares to question the acts of this earthly king. However, when God does the same thing (only with greater supervision), man says, "God can't do this! I have a free will!" Man must realize that the Sovereign God has a free will, too.

Summary

Many Christians have fallen into the "separate faith" trap. They have one faith for God's eternal salvation and another for His temporal provision. They may believe that they are eternally secure because God has promised it to be so. Yet, they might not believe that they are temporally and securely cared for. This is certainly a great inconsistency of faith. The same God has promised both eternal deliverance *and* daily sustenance. The cure for this imbalance is to focus in on and believe in the Sovereign God. He *is* in control of all things. He can be trusted for all our tomorrows. He can also be trusted day after day.

When God is trusted as the Sovereign God, great peace and security are produced in the heart of the believer. The Christian has nothing to fear. The truth of God's sovereignty does not reduce man's responsibility. Instead, when it is believed and practiced, it gives great peace, purpose, motivation, and joy.

49

We cannot be secure while we are trying to be in control. We have two choices: 1) We can live in fear and anxiety while we try to control everything around us. In doing so, we will ignore the One Who is in control of all things. 2) We can trust the Sovereign God of all things. We can believe that He is in control of all things. Worry and doubt all cease as we work and labor peacefully under His sovereign plan.

Chapter 6

Rooted and Established

Man builds and builds with great towers of much pleasure
But never is satisfied with such wealth and such treasure
For he has neglected to build on the only True Foundation
He must erect all that he does upon God's Eternal Salvation.

"As you therefore have received Christ Jesus the Lord, so walk in Him, having been firmly rooted and now being built up in Him and established in your faith, just as you were instructed, and overflowing with gratitude. See to it that no one takes you captive through philosophy and empty deception, according to the tradition of men, according to the elementary principles of the world, rather than according to Christ. For in Him all the fullness of Deity dwells in bodily form, and in Him you have been made complete, and He is the head over all rule and authority;" Colossians 2:6-10

Isn't it entertaining to drive behind the driver of another vehicle who does not know where he is going? It's quite hilarious, and can be at times, aggravating. Signal lights blink one way and then the next. Brake lights go on and off. The driver's head is on a swivel, trying to find a street sign or a building number. The car in front of you weaves hesitantly from one lane to the other. Finally, into a gas station the driver goes, seeking directions for his destination.

All this confusion was experienced because the driver was not sure of his directions or his destination. Being eternally secure in God through the Lord Jesus Christ was discussed in chapters three and four. This chapter begins a brief discussion of the practical side of developing security as a lifestyle. Knowing we are eternally secure effects the way we live. Do we travel with security? Or, do we make the journey through life in doubt and fear? The Bible is God's directions for traveling to our eternal destination.

Having roots and being established sounds like security, doesn't it? Of course it does! Being rooted and established gives one the sense of belonging that all people need. When a person is rooted and established, he is shown to be reliable. Such a person will be able to stand in times of testing.

How does one get those roots? How does one become established? As already noted, the end of the journey must be secure. Common sense illustrations of being rooted and established are also easy to see. One cannot be properly growing unless the roots are being nourished. Neither can one be established securely unless they are built upon a good foundation.

Rooted in Faith

Colossians 2:6-8 gives the <u>first</u> key into this walk of security: *rooted* in faith. The rule of conduct for the believer is to walk by faith. We know that this is true because it is only by faith that one has received Christ (verse 6). Human philosophies, deception, traditions, and worldliness (verse 8) all fit under the four enemies mentioned in Chapter One. They rob the believer of security because these elements are temporary and are not founded upon the truth.

It is not uncommon for believers to become rooted and grounded in fleshly systems. However, Galatians 3:3 says that this is indeed a foolish way of living the Christian life: "Are you so foolish? Having begun by the Spirit, are you now being perfected by the flesh?"

Confronted with the conviction of his sins, the unbelieving sinner faces the truth of who he is apart from Christ. He is also confronted with the truth of Who Christ is and what Christ's death has accomplished. After he believes and receives Christ Jesus the Lord, he has an open door to the Truth (John 14:6). From that point onward, he can walk with the Lord by faith.

Christ is the nourishing soil of truth into which the believer is planted. He is the sustainer of the soul. *The believer is to relate all of life back to the Truth (Jesus Christ).* Otherwise, insecurities develop. Then, life becomes confusing, filled with anxiety. All of life can become frightening.

Jesus Christ said that He came to set people free from the slavery caused by sin and fear. Freedom can only be experienced as one obeys the Word of God by faith. Faithful obedience does not result in austere, uncaring lives. Rather, it is a close, personal walk with the One Who is the Truth. In John 8, Jesus spoke to the many people who had come to believe Him. He defined discipleship for them. He taught that in order for believers to be classified as disciples, they must follow Him. He was and is the Truth. His Word and Truth are both seen in John 8:31,32 as being equal.

The secure behavior of the believer is therefore

planted in the soil of the Word of God. Such activity causes faith. The walk of faith is characterized by obedience to the Lord Jesus Christ and His Word.

Walking in pathways other than submissive faithful obedience to the Word of God can cause guilt and fear. Fear torments people. First John 4:18 says, "There is no fear in love; but perfect love casteth out fear: because fear hath torment. He that feareth is not made perfect in love" (KJV). Fear is not security.

As previously mentioned, faith in the Lord Jesus Christ is essential for security. How can the believer have this "walking" faith? Romans 10:17 says that faith comes through the hearing of the word of God. It is all important to have the word of God filtering through the believer as well as filtering (cleansing) the believer.

Once again, Colossians 2:6 says that the believer is to walk by faith (the same way Jesus was received). Faith is the lifestyle that is acceptable to God. It is not a mere "fire escape" from hell. It is also a secure walk based upon faithful obedience to the Scriptures.

When a person receives Christ as his personal Savior, he becomes a new creature in Christ (II Corinthians 5:17). The transformation from death into life is the greatest of all experiences for the trusting sinner. However, this salvation experience is not the end for the believer. It is a new beginning. The new Christian is free to live for Christ. Living for Christ in obedience to the Word of God is the walk of faith.

Enoch (Genesis 5) and Noah (Genesis 6-9) are two Old Testament examples of people walking by faith. They simply walked with God. Hebrews 11 lists those who are great heroes of faith. Both of these men are mentioned in Hebrews 11 as men who pleased God by their faithful walk.

Hebrews 11:5-7 -- "By faith Enoch was taken up so that he should not see death; and he was not found because God took him up; for he obtained the witness that before his being taken up he was pleasing to God. And without faith it is impossible to please Him, for he who comes to God must believe that He is, and that He is a rewarder of those who seek Him. By faith Noah, being warned by God about things not yet seen, in reverence prepared an ark for the salvation of his household, by which he condemned the world, and became an heir of the righteousness which is according to faith."

Walking with God is not a mythical lifestyle. It is not a life reserved for people with halos on top of their heads. We can still walk with the Lord today. We simply take His Word, believe it and live it. Such a lifestyle pleases God and glorifies Him. In other words, the Bible is joyfully obeyed because we believe it. It is not to be obeyed out of fear of condemnation nor as mere religious expressionism.

Pastors, missionaries, and Christian leaders are constantly bombarded with difficulties that their congregations face. Most of these problems are created by the lack of time and effort the people spend in acquiring truth. God has given His Truth to aid them in their walk of faith. When the Truth is ignored or by-passed, insecurity results. Foolish decisions are then made out of fear, anxiety, revenge, and competition.

Deuteronomy 6:5-9 -- "And you shall love the Lord your God with all your heart and with all your soul and with all your might. And these words, which I am commanding you today, shall be on your heart; and you shall teach them diligently to your sons and shall talk of them when you sit in your house and

when you walk by the way and when you lie down and when you rise up. And you shall bind them as a sign on your hand and they shall be as frontals on your forehead. And you shall write them on the doorposts of your house and on your gates."

In the above verses, God describes for His children the importance of teaching and keeping the Word of God. Bible truth is meant to be an ever present catalyst fueling the daily tasks of God's people. The purpose of this is to be a reminder of security in the Lord. Growing in the Word of God will guide believers in causing them to be rooted in faith. The nourishment of their souls will be the experience that God intended them to have. The result will be secure lives, unmovable and steadfast in the Lord Jesus Christ.

The Word of God is kept (obeyed) by those who truly love the Lord. Note that the commands of keeping and practicing the Word of God follow the command to love the Lord with all one's heart, soul, and might. Jesus simplified this in one easy statement in the New Testament (John 14:15 -- "If you love Me, you will keep My commandments.").

Everyone (lost or saved) lives by faith in something or someone. All people will be motivated to do certain things or not do certain things on the basis of what they believe. If one believes that there is a lion on his couch, he will not go into his living room. If a person believes he is ugly, he will try to compensate his belief with modification of his behavior or dress. If one believes that Christ can't save him, he will try to work his way to heaven. Christians are not the only people that have faith. However, Christians are the only people that have their faith in the *right place*, in the Lord Jesus Christ.

Therefore, the object of one's faith is extremely important. Those who say they have faith, but do not tell what their faith is in might be trusting in their own strengths or their own wishes. Such "faith" is fueled by the desires of the flesh and by the circumstances of life. Trusting fleshly desires will not lead to security.

Plants find their nourishment from the soil in which they are planted. If the roots are not healthy, the plant will not be healthy. So also, the believer must be exercising his faith in Christ. His faith must be nourished by the Word of God.

Established in Faith

The <u>second</u> key to security for the believer found in Colossians 2 is similar to the first: *established* in faith (verse 7). The believer must always be building upon the secure foundation. First Corinthians 3:11 says, "For no man can lay a foundation other than the one which is laid, which is Jesus Christ." One must be fully convinced that there is *no other* foundation upon which to build.

Many imagine that there are other foundations to build upon: feelings, education, money, marriage, friends, family, etc. Unfortunately, these things are not foundations. Rather, *they are important building blocks to be established on the One and Only Foundation, the Lord Jesus Christ.*

Jesus Christ taught these truths very plainly in Matthew 7:24-27:

"Therefore everyone who hears these words of Mine, and acts upon them, may be compared to a wise man, who built his house upon the rock. And the rain

descended, and the floods came, and the winds blew, and burst against that house; and yet it did not fall, for it had been founded upon the rock. And everyone who hears these words of Mine, and does not act upon them, will be like a foolish man, who built his house upon the sand. And the rain descended, and the floods came, and the winds blew, and burst against that house; and it fell, and great was its fall."

A house that falls down in a rainstorm is not a securely established house. A life that falls because of the trials of life is not a secure life. Remember, *reliability is tested by trials and adversity.* Failing and falling lives illustrate the very opposite of security. Note the process of establishing security as represented in Matthew 7. One must *hear* the Word of God. He must also *do* the Word of God. The obedience (doing) of the believer is to be resting on his faith (hearing) in the Word.

Attending church services, Bible conferences, seminars, retreats, and Bible classes are all good practices to maintain in one's life. However, it is necessary that these practices lead to the obedience of God's Word. If it does not, security will not be produced. An insecure life is like a house built on sand. Putting the Word of God into practice by faith is the only acceptable course of action given to the believer by God. Only then will the believer be established in a lifestyle of biblical security.

Colossians 2:6-9 opposes man's opinions and traditions. Man's traditions are not to be considered to be trustworthy foundations. Let no one be fooled by the weak things of the flesh and the foolish philosophies of the world. If these inventions of man are used for foundations, man will suffer the consequences of building upon insecurity. Only at the end of life do people realize their foolishness. They realize only too late that they've wasted their lives building sand castles. Sand castles soon wash away and are forgotten.

Truth is a Rock that does not change. Malachi 3:6 cites the immutability of God. He does not change. If God changes, then He is not true. It would mean that there was a time that He was *not* true. If God is changeable, there is absolutely no basis for security. Life would be like a game of marbles played on a ship at high seas during a fierce storm.

Man may have a problem believing in the immutability of God. On earth, everything changes. Things grow, age, and die. There is nothing on earth to compare to the eternal, changeless God of Truth.

With this in mind, it is easy to see why those who are not founded upon this Rock of Truth are trying to grab all they can before their ship goes down. Wealth, friends, family, education, fame, religion, and pleasures are the only securities these people see. Their traditions and philosophies are changeable foundations that can give a mere temporary and false security. While holding onto the solid mast of their vessel, they fail to realize that their *whole* ship is going down, and they are going down with it.

Summary

Faith is the key to becoming rooted and established. Faith is the way that we met the Lord Jesus Christ. It is also the way that we are to live. Such faith is founded upon the Rock of our redemption. It is not placed upon the sand of human philosophies and imaginations.

Faith in Christ and His Word is to be the very conviction of our lives. It is not merely an abstract thought or idea. It has substance and evidence (Hebrews 11:1). It is fully connected to life. It governs how we live. It effects our lifestyles.

We can make a choice. We can choose to believe something or someone else other than Christ. This choice will *not* lead to a life of stability. Or, we can choose to believe Christ and develop our lives based upon His word. Thus, we become rooted and established in faith.

Chapter 7

Always a Friend

Oh, so very lonely and all alone in this dark world of sin,
Searching for comfort and courage, but finding none within.
Looking above, man turns to God, to bring his quest to an end.
To be with One Who is always True, Jesus, the Faithful Friend.

You may have experienced a time when you were going to a large gathering of people where you had no acquaintances. You were going to meet a friend there. Many questions could have entered your mind while you were waiting. "Where do I sit? Should I sit down or wait at the door? What do I say? Am I properly dressed for this occasion?" Then, your friend appears and greets you. All the questions you had seem to fade into obscurity. Now, with your friend at your side, the anxiety and insecurity disappear. Joy, peace, and confidence replace the confusing thoughts that controlled you. Your friend knows the people. He knows the program. He even knows where the restrooms are. What a change has occurred with the presence of your friend!

So also it is for the believer who is secure in the Lord Jesus Christ. The believer always has a friend in all the activities of his life. This Friend has been here before. He knows the ropes. He knows all the pathways of life. He knows how to "do" life. He knows pain, sorrow, and death.

Hebrews 13:5,6 tells the believer that Jesus Christ will "never leave us nor forsake us." The purpose of this promise from the Lord is so that the believer can confidently say, "The Lord is my Helper."

The practical side of Hebrews 13:5,6 is this: God does not leave us alone in life. God never intended for us to be alone, nor lonely. We always have a Friend. Proverbs 17:17 defines the activity of a true friend: "A friend loves at all times...".

All those who have believed upon Jesus Christ are friends with God. Romans 5:1 states that the believer is no longer an enemy of God. Warfare does not exist between God and the Christian.

Peace with God is the rule for every believer. Since God is now our Friend, the Bible says that He loves us at all times (Proverbs 17:17). "All times" means that there is *never* a time that Jesus stops loving God's children, no matter what the circumstances are. This is the most important characteristic of a friend. If there are conditions placed on love from a friend, then that friendship is in jeopardy.

The greatest enemy of friendship is dishonesty. Dishonesty is a characteristic which is nonexistent within the Godhead. The integrity of God was discussed in Chapter 3, regarding the nature of God. He will forever be the True Honest Friend. He will never break His word. He can always be counted on.

The Old Testament as well as the New Testament claims Abraham to be the friend of God. However, it is not until the New Testament that we see God

representing Himself in Christ as a Friend to *all*
believers. Throughout the Gospels, Jesus (God in the
flesh) is seen as a Friend to sinners. Then, in John
15:13,15, He says:

**"Greater love has no one than this, that One lay
down His life for His friends. No longer do I call you
slaves, for the slave does not know what his master
is doing; but I have called you friends, for all things
that I have heard from My Father I have made
known to you."**

God's unconditional and undying love for the
believer is spoken of in Romans 8:31-39. Truly, He is
the Friend that loves through all the troubles and trials
of life for all time.

The practical implications of the personal security
caused by this continuous friendship has far reaching
affects in the life of every believer. The Christian can
go wherever the Lord leads Him with great confidence
and assurance.

Security and freedom from loneliness are sought
after by the world perhaps more than any other
qualities of life. There are thousands of books, tapes,
schools, etc., which promote some kind of success in
this vast area of man's needs. However, it is
experienced only by those who cultivate a constant
relationship with God through the Lord Jesus Christ.

Perhaps you have witnessed the chaos of a lost
three-year old child in a public place . Fear in the eyes,
tears, loud crying, and panic are all expressions of
extreme confusion experienced by the lost child. He is
convinced that he is hopelessly lost. At last, Mom
comes rushing to the rescue. She scoops up her child in
her arms. It is not long before the child's fears begin to

subside. Smiles and giggles replace the tears. Mom, the child's *best friend*, is present. Once again, all is well.

The second part of Hebrews 13:6 tells of another benefit for the secure Christian. "I will not be afraid. What shall man do to me?" God will never leave the believer, so the believer has nothing to fear.

We can claim that we are afraid of nothing. We can wear clothing which has words written saying that we have no fears. However, if the truths of Hebrews 13:6 are not the basis of our confidence, we will still fear. A statement denying fear does not remove fear.

Mankind gropes for all the empty and deceitful philosophies of independence, self-dependence, and autonomy. While appearing independent, he is promoting the greatest playground for fear that he can possibly face. He is alone.

Today, the false strength of aloneness is virtually worshipped. People grow up alone, live alone, and finally die alone. If they are considered to be strong, they face loneliness with all of their gallant pride, without complaining. A look at Psalm 27:1-3 reveals:

The Lord is my light and my salvation; Whom shall I fear? The Lord is the defense of my life; Whom shall I dread? When evildoers came upon me to devour my flesh, My adversaries and my enemies, they stumbled and fell. Though a host encamp against me, My heart will not fear; Though war arise against me, In spite of this I shall be confident.

These verses speak of adversaries, evildoers, a multitude of enemies, and war. Yet, this passage of Scripture is one of the greatest treatises on the topic of confidence in the Lord. If God is the light and salvation (deliverance) of the believer, what enemy is greater than He? Regardless of the circumstances, the Christian can rest securely in the Lord.

While ministering as pastor in a church in New York, I received a phone call from a friend at 1:00 AM. My friend had been visiting with an acquaintance who was practicing "black and white magic." The reason for the call was that great fear had been raised in my friend's mind. There was a need to have these fears removed. I quickly dressed and drove the three miles to my friend's house. I dealt with this "magic man" from the basis of the Word of God. I also shared my testimony of salvation. I wanted him to see and accept God's greatness and goodness.

Following this episode, my friend asked me if I was afraid. The answer was, "No, I had full confidence that the Lord was my light and my salvation." I had nothing to fear. First John 4:4 says, "You are from God, little children, and have overcome them; because greater is He who is in you than he who is in the world." My fear was conquered by confidence in the presence of my Friend, the Lord Jesus Christ. If our best Friend, Jesus Christ, is for us, who can stand against us?

One must be confident that the Lord really lives in him, that He never leaves nor forsakes him for any reason. Otherwise, great fear may be experienced. Does this mean that God is going to make sure that physical injury or even death are out of the question for those who trust Him? No, not at all!

Many times, King David faced death. In Psalm 23:4, he says, "Yea, though I walk through the valley of the shadow of death, I will fear no evil: for thou art with me; thy rod and thy staff they comfort me." The security that people have as they follow the Lord is the security of His presence, both in life and in death.

Therefore, the believer can face life and death without fear. The Christian is never alone, not even in the most alone times of life. He is never alone even at the time of death.

John 15:15 tells us of another characteristic of friendship with Christ -- communication. Jesus has made Himself known to us. We ought to make ourselves known to Him and thus experience godly fellowship with the Son of God. We should walk with Him and talk with Him.

Summary

The steps to friendship in Christ are based upon faith in Him. We must believe that God actually loves us as much as He says He does.

Carefully think of these truths regarding His friendship:

1. Jesus Christ loves us. He gave His life for us (John 15:13).
2. We are friends with Christ (John 15:15).
3. The primary characteristic of His friendship is that He loves us at *all* times, no matter what (Proverbs 17:17). Therefore, there is *never* a time that He does not love us.
4. The second characteristic of His friendship is that He is present with us at *all* times (Hebrews 13:5,6).
5. It is not possible for us to be separated from the love of God in Christ (Romans 8:31-39).
6. The third characteristic of friendship is to honestly know Jesus Christ and allow Him to openly know us (John 15:15).

Chapter 8

The Defects of Insecurity

For all that we want to be and for all the things that we need
We try to work and labor, but to the Lord we do not plead.
Yet, He is the One who graciously gives abundantly to man.
So, there is no need to be anything that is not within His plan.

Psalm 23 is the most well-loved portion of scripture in the Bible. It is read at funerals. It is expounded upon in retirement centers and nursing homes. It is preached at church services almost universally. It has been memorized perhaps more than any other six verses in the Bible. Books have been written on the topics contained within this psalm as well as on the entire psalm itself.

Why is this psalm so popular? Its popularity is largely due to the needs within mankind that are addressed within this psalm. It is a psalm of security. Jesus Christ is portrayed as the Good Shepherd, caring for His sheep. The sheep of this Shepherd depicted as safe and peaceful. All the needs of the sheep of this Good Shepherd are fulfilled.

We can become so familiar with this psalm that we may not really study it or meditate upon it. Read it again and think of all the needs that Jesus Christ meets as our Good Shepherd.

The Lord is my shepherd, I shall not want. He makes me lie down in green pastures; He leads me beside quiet waters. He restores my soul; He guides me in the paths of righteousness For His name's sake. Even though I walk through the valley of the shadow of death, I fear no evil; for Thou art with me; Thy rod and Thy staff, they comfort me. Thou dost prepare a table before me in the presence of my enemies; Thou hast anointed my head with oil; My cup overflows. Surely goodness and lovingkindness will follow me all the days of my life, And I will dwell in the house of the Lord forever. (Psalm 23)

Providence, peace, leadership, guidance, restoration, protection, comfort, approval, overflowing blessings, goodness, mercy, love, and hope are all met in Him.

All the needs of all people have been provided for in the Lord Jesus Christ. He Who is the Creator and Sustainer is also the Savior and Restorer. Not only does He do all these things for man, but He is the only One Who does so. He is kind and gentle and at the same time He is unmoving and omnipotent. He is great in His protection of His people.

Psalm 18:7-19 reveals the awesome love of God as He comes forth from glory to rescue His people. This psalm describes the passion of the Messiah (Jesus Christ), coming to save His chosen ones. His anger toward His enemies shakes the earth. His breath is filled with smoke and His words are filled with fire. Creation is affected by His powerful presence. Lightning, thunder, hail, fire, wind, clouds, and the waters all testify of the presence of the powerful passion of our Great Savior.

Our passionate God came to accomplish a personal rescue. Verses 16-19 of Psalm 18 speak of the personal rescue of the believer:

"He sent from on high, He took me; He drew me out of many waters. He delivered me from my strong enemy, And from those who hated me, for they were too mighty for me. They confronted me in the day of my calamity, But the Lord was my stay. He brought me forth also into a broad place; He rescued me, because He delighted in me."

God's love for us is passionate. He will help us, rescue us, and keep us safe. He will go through great lengths to accomplish this, even if it means that He must destroy His enemies with hatred. He will rescue us even if it causes pain to Himself.

The evidence of this kind of passionate love for us is clearly seen in the willing sacrifice of Christ on the cross of Calvary. On the cross Jesus, our Powerful Deliverer, defeated Satan, our greatest enemy. Our sins were completely paid at the expense of the life of the Perfect Lamb of God. We are safe in Him.

A thief breaks into a home in the middle of the night. He holds the peace-loving family hostage at knifepoint. The gentle parents allow the thief to take whatever he wishes so that no one in their family would be hurt. When the intruder grabs their five-year old daughter and begins to cut the child's arm, the parents become enraged. With great passion they fly to the aid of their daughter. The parents disregard their own safety. While the father grabs the knife blade in his hands, the mother reaches for an iron to use as a weapon. The parents are injured. However, the thief is quickly subdued and is nearly beaten to death in the process. This is passionate love in operation.

The destructive powers of sin (our enemy) are no match for the Great Deliverer of the souls of man. Our Savior has rescued us with great passion; He bled and died for us. Christ knows all too well the power of evil. It was He Who laid down His own life. He took all the forcefulness of sin and death upon Himself on the cross of Calvary. Jesus Christ does not have to be convinced that sin is the terrible enemy of man. We are the ones who need convincing.

In Jesus Christ we are safe and secure. In Christ, the Shepherd, we have *no needs*. When the soul of man is unfulfilled, he will look for his hunger to be satisfied. This need for satisfaction is met only in Christ. Apart from Christ, man is an extremely needy and lustful creature. He cannot say, "I shall not want," when Christ is not his Shepherd.

Many (and it seems it is the majority of people) try to find fulfillment of life and satisfaction for the soul in places other than in the Lord Jesus Christ. Because these other things *cannot* satisfy man's genuine needs, a continued lack of peace and comfort will be their experience. This causes persistent character defects. These defects are represented by a constant void in the lives of people who do not have Christ as the Good Shepherd. Therefore, the opposite is also true: "The Lord is not my shepherd; I want and I want and I want, and I am never fulfilled and satisfied."

With the Lord as our Shepherd, the guardian of our souls, we do not have to open our lives up to wickedness. We can be completely fulfilled in the Lord Jesus Christ. Surely, this is the abundant life Jesus was speaking of in John 10:10.

Life without the Shepherd is empty. Emptiness in the life of man leaves his soul open to be filled with many evil things. God warns His people of this emptiness in His Word. Jesus spoke of the dangers of an empty life in Luke 11: 24-26:

"When the unclean spirit goes out of a man, it passes through waterless places seeking rest, and not finding any, it says, 'I will return to my house from which I came.' And when it comes, it finds it swept and put in order. Then it goes and takes along seven other spirits more evil than itself, and they go in and live there; and the last state of that man becomes worse than the first."

The following ten items are only a partial list of characteristics of unfulfilled, empty lives. Life without the Shepherd is characterized by these ten defects:

The Defect of Improper Worship

If the *Lord* is not man's Shepherd, then someone or something else must be. When man becomes his own shepherd/provider, his worship will be directed toward himself. He has fooled himself into thinking that he is the controller of his own destiny. "God helps those who help themselves," is the excuse people use to refuse God the position of worship He deserves. Under the guise of "helping themselves," they may excuse the sins of idolatry and covetousness.

I have thought it interesting that someone might claim to be a "self-made man." This means he is taking the credit for the way he has turned out. It also means that he is taking the credit for all of his mistakes. Such an attitude of independence dismisses any need or desire to worship God.

Covetousness is the rule of life for those who do not experience the providence of God in Christ. Worshipping the created thing rather than the Creator is spoken of in Romans 1:25. The Scriptures accuse those who practice such worship of idolatry.

The desire to have *things* can become so strong that people may find temporary security in their possessions. The craving for earthly possessions can easily become uncontrolled, overbalanced, and overwhelming. When desires become this large, they are called lusts. A lifestyle of covetousness is the defective result of such continued lusts.

Covetousness and idolatry are equated as one and the same in Colossians 3:5: "Mortify therefore your members which are upon the earth; fornication, uncleanness, inordinate affection, evil concupiscence, and covetousness, which is idolatry" (KJV). In truth, a covetous person can say, "My desire for things is my shepherd and I want more and more."

The Lord, our Shepherd, is our Provider. Providence is the chief function of the shepherd as he cares for his flock. All too often, we are not convinced of this truth. Our behavior shows that our faith is not in the God of providence. We may feel that *we* are the providers. At other times, we simply do not believe that God *is* providing for our needs. This usually happens when our desires supersede our God-given needs. Idolatrous (coveting) attitudes are commonly accepted as our normal American lifestyle.

The prayer life of the believer can be used as a spiritual measuring rod. What the Christian prays for can reveal whether or not he is a covetous person.

Often, covetousness is the singular focus of the prayer life of the Christian (James 4:3). Most prayers offered to God are concerned about what people have or what they do not have.

Jesus Christ taught us to pray, "Give us this day our daily bread." We ought to seek the Lord for our daily needs. However, Jesus did not teach us to pray, "Give us more and more to satisfy our lusts."

We are to seek God for our daily needs so that His divine purposes may be met in our lives. While we enjoy the physical blessings God bestows upon us, we need to remember that such blessings are not the end of God's work in and through our lives. His desire is that we become spiritually fruitful as a result of all His bounteous work in our lives.

Prayer ought to be offered in trust to the One Who is the Great Provider of all things. Often, the health and wealth of believers are prayed for above the spiritual needs that they have. *God is Divine Providence. He alone is worthy of worship!*

The Defect of Anxiety

Two teachings are necessary to bring peace into our lives while we make decisions. The first teaching is the teaching of trusting God for the results. There can be no peace for the one who is not trusting in the Lord. Unbelief is sin and will result in anxiety. Isaiah 48:22 says, "There is no peace for the wicked." Life merely becomes one crisis after another, one worry after another. For the one who worries, confidence in God is often replaced by confusion.

Skepticism and futility are characteristics of a life that is submerged in doubt and fear. Jesus Christ, the Prince of Peace is the only One Who can free people from such anxieties. Trusting Him is the only road to true peace.

A Christian may be looking for a place to live. He may be plagued by not knowing what would be the right room or apartment to rent, or the right house to purchase. Another believer may wonder if the Lord would guide him in choosing to buy a new car. Both may be very sincere about trying to discern God's will in these matters. However, both can suffer from undo stress and anxiety while making their decisions. Both could be trying *to govern the outcome of their decisions by making the right choice.*

This is something that *we* cannot do; only God can do this. No one else can declare the end from the beginning. Isaiah 46:9,10 says:

"Remember the former things long past, For I am God, and there is no other; I am God, and there is no one like Me, Declaring the end from the beginning. And from ancient times things which have not been done, Saying, 'My purpose will be established, And I will accomplish all My good pleasure';"

While it is important to make wise choices in our lives with the help of the Lord, such a process should never lead to stress. It is not possible for us to determine the result of anything. Only God can do that. We may become displeased with the choice we have made. When this happens, a learning experience has been placed in our lives. God led us through that choice to teach us valuable lessons that we would not have otherwise learned. Believers can put themselves through unnecessary worry at crossroads in their lives. Such worry is in direct opposition to the "lying down in green pastures" described in Psalm 23.

Planning is consistent with a godly way of life. God plans. So should the believer. However, all plans should be submitted to the Lord with this prayer, "Nevertheless, not what I will, but Thy will be done."

God can and does interrupt our plans any time and any way He desires. The Christian who is trusting the Lord will find peace in these interruptions, rather than anxiety. He can experience peace during interruptions because he knows that God has the best plan for his life. As discussed in Chapter Five, God is in control of *all* things. Our confidence needs to be placed in Him, rather than in our own ability to make decisions. God's plans are *never* defective.

God told Isaiah to prophesy to Israel. Isaiah was also told that no one would listen to him. He obeyed the Lord even though He knew that his work would appear fruitless before man.

Job lost his possessions, his family, his health, and his friends. He spoke of how the Lord can give and take away at any moment and for any reason He sees fit. Yet, he would not speak evil of God. He knew that God was in charge of the results.

As these Old Testament saints learned, we need to willingly submit to the Lord while we make decisions. Then, and only then, the peace of God will be the rule to guide us in all we do. Without the reality of willing submission, insecurities will be caused by our own desire to "declare the end from the beginning."

Shortly before our daughter's fifteenth birthday, she developed a seizure disorder. Neurologists prescribed many kinds of anti-convulsive medicines. These did not cause the seizures to stop. Over the course of eight and a half years, she saw neurologists, eyeurdologists, and had numerous CT and MRI scans.

She went through many changes in medicine and ate a diet of seaweed and kidney beans. The seizures continued and became debilitating.

Every avenue of treatment had been exhausted until the only course left was brain surgery. She went through two surgeries to remove one benign tumor. After the second surgery, she finally emerged seizure free.

At each step of this long process, with many bills and times of despair, we sought the Lord. Nothing seemed to work, even though we followed all the doctors' orders explicitly. We spoke to a medical research scientist friend who had been helping to find doctors for our daughter. When I relayed the entire history of our daughter's problems to him, he spoke with other doctors who reviewed what we had done. They all agreed. The treatment that we had followed was exactly the one they would have taken, given the same set of circumstances.

We did not know at the time that God was leading us in our decision-making process. Nevertheless, He *was* leading us. We simply trusted Him each agonizing step of the way, even though we did not have any assurance of the results. We had even come to the place of accepting that one of the results may be a daughter with seizures for the rest of her life. We learned what it meant to trust the Lord and to be secure while doing so. God was, and is in control of all things. Looking back over this trial, we have to admit that we did not know what we were doing. We also believed that many of the doctors did not know what they were doing. However, we praise the Lord that He knew what He was doing!

The second essential teaching which governs our

peace during times of decision is the presence of God. The presence of God while we make decisions is crucial. In Matthew 18:15-20 we are told the importance of the presence of the Lord during times when we need to make decisions. This passage of Scripture maps out the program for church discipline. Church discipline is one of the most difficult decisions that a church can make. It is to be executed as a last resort with extreme love and understanding, yet in firmness.

Jesus' teaching of the disciplinary process ends with the great assurance of His presence. In verse 20, He says, "For where two or three have gathered together in My name, there I am in their midst." Most people take this as a verse describing fellowship. It is not.

Others mistake this verse to be a prayer promise verse. They feel that God is promising to answer their prayers if two or more people are agreeing on a particular prayer request. Prayer is not the theme of this passage of Scripture. The central theme of these verses is "how to make wise decisions which affect the work of the ministry."

Matthew 18:20 is an assurance verse. It means that when Christians are making decisions based upon sound biblical principles and standards, they can be assured of the peaceful presence of Christ. If they are *not* making decisions based upon biblical principles, they will have *no* assurance of His presence. The only possible result will be unwise decisions made out of anxiety. The "two or three" who are in agreement show the necessity of proper biblical communication and understanding.

Trusting God for the results and walking in His

presence takes away the defect of anxiety. One who does so is at peace and is truly "lying down in green pastures."

The Defect of Confusion

Divine leadership and guidance becomes greatly limited to the one straying outside the Shepherd's fold. He becomes a wandering sheep and does not know where to go. He is uncertain in all things that he does. His *self*-governed course of acceptable action can be traditionally applauded by his peers. However, such approval only means that groups of people can find false security in their numbers.

Without leadership from the Lord, man *must* find leadership from another source. That other source will always be a substandard, even if a multitude of people are in agreement with such a standard. Confusion will always be the end product of such leadership.

A sheep gone astray is defined for us in Isaiah 53:6: "All of us like sheep have gone astray, Each of us has turned to his own way; But the Lord has caused the iniquity of us all to fall on Him." Going astray is equal to turning to our own ways. We might look and act secure. However, if we are merely trusting in our own strength and ingenuity, we are greatly limited.

Submission to the Good Shepherd will produce characteristics which represent Him. Christ is manifested by Christians who are living in His righteousness. Paths of righteousness are the only paths into which our Good Shepherd will leads us.

The Defect of Corruption

There is no restoration for the one who has given

himself over to the life outside the sheepfold. The only place of restoration and renewal is within the secure gates of the Good Shepherd. All other places bring a defective life of corruptibility. Forgiveness leads to security while remaining unforgiven genders a life filled with degeneration. In no way does an unrestored sheep cease to be a sheep. However, in every sense of the word, he is a sheep that needs to be brought back into the security of the fold. This process is called restoration.

Emptiness and uselessness are defects of the decaying lifestyle of people outside the security of the Shepherd Who brings restoration. Sheep wandering outside the fold may be considered to be wild. Wild sheep are always in danger of predators. Therefore, it would be foolish for a sheep to live in the wild without a shepherd. Foolish sheep place themselves outside the secure protection of the Good Shepherd. They do not heed His Word.

Satan walks about as a roaring lion, seeking whom he may devour (I Peter 5:8). The whole lifestyle of believers outside the protection of the Shepherd differs from those who are in safety. The straying sheep must constantly be taking care of his own needs and his own security. *The whole emphasis of a wandering sheep turns to survival, rather than service.*

This is tragic. Christ has set us on a course of restoration. The path on which He leads us is the path of restoration and life, rather than emptiness, futility, decay, and death. The believer is out of place when embracing a treacherous lifestyle outside the fold.

As believers in Christ, we are trustees, stewards. We are entrusted with a new life in Christ. The origin of our new life is in the resurrected Shepherd. The end of our new life is also in Him. The process between the beginning (salvation) and the end (eternity) is to be one of restoration. As trustees of this new life, we are to have a lifestyle of usefulness and ministry based upon that trust. We need to be developing a way of life that is consistent with life and restoration. Such development is found only in Christ, the Restorer of our souls.

The Defect of Danger

Away from the Lord Jesus Christ lies the path of danger. Destruction awaits those who are trying to live the Christian life without Christ. What a contradiction in terms!

Protection is in the hands of the kind and powerful Shepherd. He holds the rod and the staff: the rod to beat off the enemies and the staff to pull the sheep into safety. People have a tendency to flirt with the danger of sin, being enticed by the excitement and pleasure of it. Christ, the love of the believer's life, keeps us focused upon Him. In doing so, the believer remains secure in the deepest snake-infested jungle of Africa or in the most drug-filled ghetto of a large inner city. Safety of person, family, or country does not rest in the hands of the individual, but rather, in the hands of the Almighty Shepherd.

The Defect of Despair

The weak and self-serving elements of the world can never bring encouragement to the believer. Often believers are fooled by the quantity and the glittering quality of such weak and beggarly elements. Yet, only Christ can comfort the sorrowing heart with His love and assurance.

Temporary flashes of happiness can occur through various accomplishments and obtained kindnesses. However, people are to be painfully reminded that the sum of their lives is not based upon what they have or what they do (Luke 12:15 -- And He said to them, "Beware, and be on your guard against every form of greed; for not even when one has an abundance does his life consist of his possessions.").

True lasting encouragement can come only from God. This is very humbling, yet very true. All of our accomplishments cannot fill the void of needed advocacy from the Lord. There is nothing anyone possesses apart from the graciousness of God (I Corinthians 4:7 -- For who regards you as superior? And what do you have that you did not receive? But if you did receive it, why do you boast as if you had not received it?).

Pride takes us outside the safety of humility. Humility keeps us near the Good Shepherd. We are keenly aware of our need for Him when we are humble. Pride refuses His help. The Lord's presence is and should be our comfort. Without the Shepherd's presence, we lose sight of His purpose for our lives. Therefore, we view our lives with despair, vanity, and hopelessness. However, the trusting Christian is comforted by the rod and staff of his Good Shepherd.

The Defect of Rejection

The secure believer knows that God has accepted him. Therefore, he is not always looking for God to re-approve him. The believer's works are always being weighed by himself and by others according to the

Word of God. Yet, the believer himself has been completely and graciously accepted by God.

Acceptance with God was never based upon what the Christian did or what he was going to do. God's acceptance of the Christian was never based upon the believer's perception nor God's perception of the size, the intensity, nor the amount of his sins. *His acceptance by God was and is based upon his personal faith in Christ.* The same rule is in effect after a person becomes a child of God (John 1:12). After one is saved, he does not continue to work to be accepted by God.

Those who do not believe in Christ are outside the Shepherd's fold. They are always trying to prove themselves to God and man. They have been rejected, condemned ("... he that believeth not is condemned already, because he hath not believed in the name of the only begotten Son of God" -- John 3:18, KJV). So, they try and try and try again. They compare their deeds to the deeds of others. They may believe that if they can do something good or be somebody great, then God might accept them.

Second Kings 5 contains the story of Naaman, the leper. He desperately wanted to do something that would make him acceptable to Elisha's God. He could not. His greatness as a warrior and leader were rejected. His gifts for Elisha were turned away. Finally, he heeded the simple counsel of his servants. There was no acceptable thing he could do. He had to humbly receive the simplicity of the command by faith, "Wash and be clean."

Similarly, we are accepted by God upon the basis of being washed by the blood of Jesus Christ. There is no rejection for the believer in Christ. In the presence of the rejection of our enemies, we are accepted by

82

God. God even prepares a table of provision and fellowship (Psalm 23:5) for us during great times of adversity.

Clearly, we show greater spiritual growth during times of trials and tests than at any other times in our lives. This is caused by God's constant acceptance of us through Christ. The basis of God's acceptance of us is Christ's perfect work on our behalf. It is not based upon our failures and successes. When our enemies reject us, we turn to our Heavenly Father. We find that the table of fellowship has already been set for us to enjoy.

The Defect of Destitution

My father was an alcoholic and a gambler. Thus, while growing up in our home, we were convinced that we were a deprived and destitute family. We had one good set of clothes (with patches), and one set not so good (with holes). Food was often scarce. We had running water; we had to run to the stream to "fetch" it. A number of times, we ran out of heating fuel in the winter time. Abuse, beatings, hatred, selfishness, and stress were continuous. Our home was dominated by tension.

In the midst of this, my mother (who was a Christian) manifested that she was the richest person on earth. Her source of strength from the Lord was the bright hope of our lives. In the midst of all adversity, there was always praise in her mouth, a smile in her eyes, and a song in her heart. Her faith and security from the Lord carried her through the deepest trials a woman could bear for herself as well as for her children. Truly, she had the joy of the Lord in her life.

My mother's joy did not come from our home. There was an outside influence. This influence was the Lord Jesus Christ, manifesting Himself in her life as the "oil of gladness" (Psalm 45:7; Hebrews 1:9).

Those who do not have the Lord as their Shepherd live in extreme poverty and despair. Unbelievers do not know how destitute they are as they compare themselves to others regarding the things of the flesh. Those who have Christ as their Shepherd have the overflowing cup (Psalm 23:5) of blessings from the hand of God.

The Defect of Cruelty

Was David really telling the truth when he said that without a doubt, goodness and lovingkindness would follow him *all* the days of his life (Psalm 23:6)? What about the adulterous incident with Bathsheba? How about the death of their first son? What happened with Absalom? What about the judgment against Israel due to David's foolish numbering of the people? Were these the events of goodness and mercy to which David was referring?

God is sometimes accused of cruelty and harshness. Insurance companies have the reputation of referring to hurricanes, tornadoes, earthquakes, and floods as "acts of God." The concept is plain: "Since man has no control over these things, God must have done them." The argument is: God has control over some things and man has control over the other things. Therefore, God may be viewed as cruel and man may view himself as kind. If God is looked upon as cruel and harsh, the words "goodness and mercy" (Psalm 23), would be in opposition.

The chief problem with this concept is that men have a different agenda than the one God has. If God does not fulfill the agendas of men, then He is considered by men to be mean, cruel, and useless (the agnostic approach to God).

When Christ came into the world, the opinion of many was that He came to break the yoke of the Roman Empire over the nation of Israel. However, the plan that Christ fulfilled was that of His Heavenly Father's: to die for the sins of man. This was an entirely different plan than what man had envisioned.

God is the One Who is providing security at all times, even in times of great catastrophes. When God is perceived in this light, one sees goodness and mercy all the days of his life. Without this perception, God is looked upon as cruel and useless.

We become tired and worn under the load of caring throughout life. God never fails. In the midst of all catastrophes, He remains sovereign and He remains kind. He is both wise and good at all times. He takes us through the trials of life.

Isaiah 43:1,2 -- But now, thus says the Lord, your Creator, O Jacob, And He who formed you, O Israel, "Do not fear, for I have redeemed you; I have called you by name; you are Mine! When you pass through the waters, I will be with you; And through the rivers, they will not overflow you. When you walk through the fire, you will not be scorched, Nor will the flame burn you."

God knows exactly what we need in this sin-cursed world. He knows that above all things, we need His abiding presence through this harsh life. The greatest of all cruelties is to go through life alone. No matter how good or how bad life may seem, the believer has the assurance of God's presence. All who belong to the Lord will arrive safely in heaven with their Redeemer forever.

The Defect of Hopelessness

The eternal security of the believer (discussed in Chapter 3) gives the hope that is necessary for living today. Often, helpless people feel they have no reason to exist. They may believe that things are not going to get any better. On the other hand, believers in Christ are neither helpless nor hopeless. Christians know that all will be made right in eternity. They can struggle through *all* difficulties because of this knowledge, even the difficulties of death.

Without the secure hope of eternal life in Christ, man is a miserable creature (I Corinthians 15:19). He is to be pitied, since his existence is entirely confined to the temporary unfulfilling life he presently possesses.

In I Thessalonians 4:13-18, God encourages us with the great hope of eternal life and the immanent rapture of the church. First century Christians were dying by natural causes and by persecution. To the Thessalonian believers, life seemed hopeless. In the light of these terrifying circumstances, God was assuring His people that Jesus could return for them at any time. The teaching of eternal life and the immanent return of Christ gave the believers great hope and security.

Believers have the promise of eternal life, to live with the Lord forever. Of all people on the earth, Christians have the privilege to walk through life as they look forward to heaven. They can live, trusting that God's promise will be completed. They know that they will dwell with the Lord forever. This frees the believer from despair and hopelessness. Without this hope, people are indeed hopeless.

Summary

Because the Lord is our Shepherd, we have no true needs. We do not have to be filled with the fears of this world. We do not have to envy others for their wealth and talents. We do not have to be filled with pride (We are sheep). The idolatry of covetousness is not necessary. We have the One Who is taking the best care of us.

In Christ, worldly defects can be taken away. Without Christ, the defects not only remain, but also can become controlling and obnoxious. Jesus Christ, our Good Shepherd brings genuine fulfillment which enables His people to change for the better.

The fulfillment of all our insufficiencies is found in our Good Shepherd Who gently leads us by the peaceful waters. All of our personal problems and deepest needs are met in the Lord Jesus Christ. Truly, the Shepherd has set us free to be His sheep.

Chapter 9

Security: The Basis For Fruitfulness

Wasting life with all its pleasures, we lose so much right from the start.
But God has spoken, His Word is true, He moves upon the heart.
By obeying Him we find great joy, growing forth from the Root,
Close to God we increase each day, bringing forth His precious fruit.

The believer is constantly reminded to manifest the characteristics of the Lord Jesus Christ. He tries and he fails and then he tries again. He is told that as he is being Christ-like, he is bearing spiritual fruit. Hopefully, he learns that all he needs to do is to keep the garden nourished and the fruit will grow.

Galatians 5:19-23 contrasts the works of the flesh and the fruit of the Holy Spirit. Although it may be difficult for many to accept, the believer cannot grow the fruit of the Spirit by trying harder. Only God can grow this fruit. It is grown, not by trying, but by trusting God.

As covered in Chapter 6 (Rooted and Established), faith is the key. But, wait! Faith is also one of the aspects of the fruit to be grown in our lives (Galatians 5:22). This sounds like a circular argument. One has to have faith to be secure, but this faith does not come from himself. It is a gift from God, yet, people are commanded to believe.

The answer to this seeming paradox is found in the Scriptures. Romans 10:17 tells us that faith comes to a person as he hears the Word of God. Faith occurs as the Holy Spirit implants the truths of the Word of God in a person's heart.

Biblical faith is strong because it is placed in Christ. The reason for strong faith is not because *we* are the ones who are doing the believing. It is strong because of the One Who is believed. Believers may be praised for their steadfast faith in God. It may be said that they are immovable in their trust. This shows the power of God and His Word, not the power of man. It is God's Word that is alive and active. God's Word causes faith. Faith then causes the believer to operate according to Bible truth (Hebrews 4:12). This is called a life of faith, or, faithfulness.

Psalm 1:2,3 speaks of the relationship between the Word of God and fruitfulness. This relationship is a progression of:

1) delighting in the Word of God,
2) continuously meditating upon the Word of God,
3) growing from the nourishment of the Word of God,
4) being fruitful and prosperous according to the Word of God.

As discussed in Chapter 6, faith is the key to being rooted and established. Faith is essential to be secure (rooted and established) in the Lord. Faith is also necessary in order for the fruit of the Spirit to be evident in the life of the believer.

When plants are transplanted from one place to another, a good root system is necessary. If the root system is inadequate, the ability of the plant to bear fruit is in jeopardy. In some cases, the plant has all it can do to survive.

The same is true of believers. A believer who is not properly rooted and grounded in the Word of God will not have true interest in bearing fruit. His interest will be self-centered. Rather than being concerned about bearing spiritual fruit, his concern will be for his own survival.

Therefore, security in the Word of God has a direct result upon the fruitfulness of the believer. Note the effects of security and insecurity upon the fruit of the Spirit of Galatians 5:22,23.

Love

Love is not able to be shown from the insecure heart. The concern of insecure people is to satisfy small, guarded portions of their own personal needs.

Insecure people are constantly grasping for all the love and affection they can possibly get. They are consumed with selfish feelings and the desire for possessions. In this state of mind they have no desire for sharing in a sacrificial manner. Their own comforts become all-important. While there may be some attempts to give, there are always strings attached to the gift. Such people are often offended that no one has recognized their "generosity." Their attempts to act lovingly will usually be outward in appearance. The character of such outward manifestations is more "approval seeking" than giving.

However, the one who is secure in the Lord by faith through the Word will be able to give of himself without reservation. He knows God and continues to know Him. He knows God's love. He has received it and dwells in it as a way of life. He is secure in God's love. He has incorporated God's love into his own life by faith. God, in turn, can love others through the believer who has this knowledge of security.

It is the natural tendency for the healthy apple tree to bring forth good apples. Like the well-rooted and fruitful tree (Psalm 1), the secure Christian will have a natural tendency to manifest the love of God to others. II Corinthians 5:14,18-20 tells us that the motivation to share Christ is due to the love of Christ in our hearts:

"For the love of Christ controls us, having concluded this, that one died for all, therefore all died; Now all these things are from God, who reconciled us to Himself through Christ, and gave us the ministry of reconciliation, namely, that God was in Christ reconciling the world to Himself, not counting their trespasses against them, and He has committed to us the word of reconciliation. Therefore, we are ambassadors for Christ, as though God were entreating through us; we beg you on behalf of Christ, be reconciled to God."

Without the love of Christ in our hearts, we may be able share God's word to the lost. God may use that word to save the lost. However, it is better to realize that God wants to love unbelievers through us. It is more than a Christian duty. It is Christ in us, loving people. The love of Christ for us compels us to share this great salvation with others.

The secure believer will be growing in love as he allows Christ to love him. Somewhat surprisingly, insecure people are afraid to receive love. It is too obligating for them. Love threatens their selfishness.

Christ's love destroys selfishness and makes the believer secure. Possessing Christ's love brings security into the believer's life. Fear vanishes. Secure in Christ's love, the believer can freely love others without reservation.

Joy

Insecurity results in weak Christians. The joy of the Lord has always been the strength of the believer (Nehemiah 8:10). When the foundation and the chief desires of one's life are placed upon the moveable sand of possessions and circumstances, joy can never be attained. There will always be others who will have more things. Others can always be found that seem to have less difficult lives. Such people will not be trusting the Lord, but will be trusting things. Life then becomes an uncertain game of survival for those who do not have security in the Lord Jesus Christ.

Isn't victory fun? When I played college soccer, we won two league championships. They were both times of great joy and happiness. We were victorious. The season before the two championships was a season of defeat. We lost the championship game in sudden death overtime. The final score was 1-0. The point is, victory and joy go together. Defeat and sadness also go together.

Victorious joy is a unique characteristic of the Christian life. Luke 10:17-20 tells the story identifying the lasting precious joy of the Christian:

"And the seventy returned with joy, saying, 'Lord, even the demons are subject to us in Your name.' And He said to them, 'I was watching Satan fall from heaven like lightning. Behold, I have given you authority to tread upon serpents and scorpions, and

over all the power of the enemy, and nothing shall injure you. Nevertheless do not rejoice in this, that the spirits are subject to you, but rejoice that your names are recorded in heaven.'"

The above verses tell that the disciples were involved in the greatest circumstances that God had allowed them to experience. They were casting out demons in the name of Jesus Christ. What could be more exciting than to see the power of God working through their ministries!? They were rejoicing in the great victories that they were experiencing. With the authority of Christ, they were defeating the enemy, and the enemy was fleeing! They saw first hand the great power of God over evil. When they shared their joy and excitement to the Lord, He wisely cautioned them.

We need to be cautioned, too. Great events are not the source of our joy. Joy is not caused by our works, our deeds, our victories, or the things that we have. The accomplishments that are granted to us (no matter how immense they are) are not the source of our joy. Rather, we are to rejoice that our names are written down in heaven. *This is true and final joy!*

Mountain top experiences cause great wonder and awe in our lives. Yet, lasting joy is found only in the eternal deliverance we have in the Lord Jesus Christ. We can anticipate eternity with Christ because our names are written in heaven. All mountain top experiences fade with time. The placement of the believer's name in heaven is permanent.

Those who are not sure that their names are written in heaven are always searching for greater and higher mountain tops. Their security is based upon the joy of having or doing something. Many people have their religious outlook based upon this philosophy of joy. Insecure Christians constantly wonder if Jesus really loves them. They are not always having great encounters of victory in circumstances. Security placed in the movable standards of circumstances will not lead to lasting joy.

The Lord's Table (communion) is to be a time of rejoicing. It is an expression of *the* mountain top experience for the believer. At that time, the believer specifically remembers that Christ died for his sins. He remembers that his name is written in heaven.

Telling the gospel to others is the same source of steadfast joy. While doing so, the believer remembers that his name is inscribed in glory by the Son of God. Personal testimony to the fact of God's redemption serves as a constant joyful reminder of the believer's home in glory.

Every evening, the believer is to remember to confess his sins before the Lord. We are commanded in Ephesians 4:26 ... "do not let the sun go down on your anger." At that time, he rejoices in the forgiveness of being a child of God. Rather than joy being based upon *having* something or *doing* something, it is based upon *being* a forgiven and cleansed child of God (I John 1:9).

When believers look for greater joy than this simple yet powerful realization, they minimize the sacrifice made for them by the Lord Jesus Christ. This sacrifice is the greatest event for the believer. It is the greatest event because of the extent of God's love manifested for His children. It is also the greatest event because of the permanent nature of the heavenly gift given by the Lord.

If the death of Christ is not the greatest event for the Christian, joy will quickly vanish from his heart. The Holy Spirit of God dwells in the believer.   When the death Christ is minimized by the Christian, the Holy Spirit is grieved. When He is sad, the believer will be sad.

How does joy make the believer strong? Fellowship with God through constant reminders of being in His family and experiencing His forgiveness makes strong believers. Joyful fellowship can only be experienced by those who are being cleansed. Believers who ignore the sacrificial death of Christ will be drifting from one circumstance to another. False joy will not strengthen their wandering hearts.

Peace

Have you ever watched a coyote in captivity at the zoo? The animal has no peace. He constantly moves from one end of the cage to the other, looking for a way to escape. He has lost his freedom and security to roam the hillsides.

One cannot experience peace without security. The two terms are almost synonymous. People without security may feel like that coyote. They wander back and forth in life, wishing that they could somehow go somewhere, even anywhere. They do not want to make any decision to get themselves out of their predicament. Obedience to the Lord has been ruled out as being "too confining." So, they plunge their lives into the confinement of insecurity by their disobedience and rebellion.

For the believer, the war with God is over (Romans 5:1 -- "Therefore having been justified by faith, we have peace with God through our Lord Jesus Christ"). The believer is no longer an enemy of God nor is God an enemy of the believer. Knowing this to be true, it is vital for the believer to know his new-found Friend. He needs to live at peace with the One Who is the creator and giver of peace.

Philippians 4:6-9 --"Be anxious for nothing, but in everything by prayer and supplication with thanksgiving let your requests be made known to God. And the peace of God, which surpasses all comprehension, shall guard your hearts and your minds in Christ Jesus. Finally, brethren, whatever is true, whatever is honorable, whatever is right, whatever is pure, whatever is lovely, whatever is of good repute, if there is any excellence and if anything worthy of praise, let your mind dwell on these things. The things you have learned and received and heard and seen in me, practice these things; and the God of peace shall be with you."

The formula for the believer to pursue the peace of God is simple. (1) Talk to the Lord, (2) Meditate upon His goodness, and (3) Obey Him. When this simple formula is followed, the peace promised from God will be experienced by the believer.

As with all the commands of the Word of God, simplicity is not synonymous with success. Simplicity merely means that these commands are easy to understand. The believer has fleshly tendencies to worry, to take things into his own hands, to refuse to pray, to think about things that are not pleasing to the Lord, and to disobey God. While building on these sinful premises, the fruit of peace and security will never be experienced.

Patience

True patience always includes endurance. Job is

cited in the book of James as a man of great endurance. James 5:11 -- "Behold, we count those blessed who endured. You have heard of the endurance of Job and have seen the outcome of the Lord's dealings, that the Lord is full of compassion and is merciful."

What was it that kept Job going? It was the security he found in the Lord. He said in Job 19:25,26 -- "And as for me, I know that my Redeemer lives, And at the last He will take His stand on the earth. Even after my skin is destroyed, Yet from my flesh I shall see God." The truth of knowing that his future was secure kept him strong and enduring in the present.

Just as Job knew, the believer knows he has a secure place in heaven with His Redeemer. Therefore, he can be patient in all things. All believers will someday see Christ, their blessed Redeemer, forever.

We know that we are on the winning side. Victory is ours in Christ. We will be safe on heaven's shore, walking with our wonderful Savior. The knowledge of our future security causes us to patiently endure the trials and tests of everyday life.

Goodness

As discussed in Chapter 8, the Christian has no reason to be unkind, harsh, and without good manners. He is secure in his Shepherd. The Good Shepherd has provided for all his needs. A harsh sinful world, cursed by God (Genesis 3), awaits to consume the kind Christian. Satan (II Corinthians 4:3,4) opposes the Holy Spirit's fruit of kindness and goodness.

When Jesus taught people to turn the other cheek, he was teaching kindness and goodness in a world of antagonism and cruelty. How can one open up his life to others, knowing that someone is ready to step on his heart? The answer is simple. Without security in the Lord, all other people will always be looked upon as opponents. They are a threat to do harm to those who are merciful. If people are providing for themselves, competition is inevitable. Goodness and kindness are often discarded so one may "survive."

When God is looked upon as the Shepherd and Provider, His people can afford to manifest goodness and kindness. When this happens, other people appear to be poor and destitute, rather than threatening. Those people once perceived as a threat, appear needy.

People are extremely needy without the Shepherd/Provider. Their own spiritual poverty will not allow them to offer the fruitfulness of goodness to others. Without security, kindness and goodness are absent. Insecure motives of selfishness and fear will not allow others to threaten them. Jesus Christ cannot be represented by selfishness and fear.

Acts 10:38 tells us that Jesus "went about doing good." This was His reputation and is in contrast to the charlatans of His times as well as today. In Acts 6 and in the pastoral epistles of I & II Timothy and Titus, there is great emphasis on goodness. God's people are to have this reputation. This is true especially of church leaders.

Church leaders are to possess the God-given qualities of goodness, mercy, and kindness. The pastoral epistles mentioned above gives these as qualifications which God uses for His work through pastors and deacons. Securely manifesting these characteristics is essential for proper leadership within the local church. Secure church leadership will be discussed more fully in Chapter 14.

Faithfulness

I enjoy taking a trip to the ocean or to a large lake on a very windy day. The waves are being tossed to and fro and the wind driven mist stings as it hits my face. Not one drop of water is secured to anything. The composition of water is such that it always follows the easiest path.

This is also true of people living in insecurity. They will always take the route of least resistance. The fruit of the Spirit as manifested by faithfulness cannot be entered into without security. James 1:5-8 says,

"But if any of you lacks wisdom, let him ask of God, who gives to all men generously and without reproach, and it will be given to him. But let him ask in faith without any doubting, for the one who doubts is like the surf of the sea driven and tossed by the wind. For let not that man expect that he will receive anything from the Lord, being a double-minded man, unstable in all his ways."

Faithfulness has become a lost way of life in our modern society of ease. Many prayer meetings are filled with requests for God to make life easy. Learning experiences of faithfulness are cast aside for feelings of ease and comfort. Instead of asking the Lord to make us faithful, we ask Him to make life easy.

Membership in churches is considered to be optional. If people do not like the programs, a particular person, or the pastor's style of preaching, they move to another church. Sometimes, Christians stop attending churches altogether.

Marriages are split because of the unfaithfulness of infidelity. Loyalty to a boss or to a company is commonly cited as a sign of weakness. Sports teams have no loyalty to their fans and leave town at the beckoning of the highest bidder. Dollar signs often govern people's faithfulness rather than a peaceful relationship with God.

Faithfulness is related to steadfastness, not being moved by false teaching. It is loyalty, honesty, and the act of standing firm. However, if the ground on which one is standing is not firm (money, feelings, lust, people, relationships, education, peers, etc.), God's spiritual fruit of faithfulness will not grow. Unfaithfulness will often be the rule of life for those building on false foundations.

In Matthew 7, Jesus taught that if one builds his life on His teachings, they would be like a house with a firm foundation. Such a house would be steadfast. It would be faithful to its owner. It would not be pushed around nor destroyed by the torrents of water. Security is clearly represented by faithfulness.

Gentleness and Meekness

The fruit of gentleness and meekness is taken advantage of by ungodly people. The reason Christians can be meek and gentle is that they know that God is taking care of everything. Meekness is experienced when Christians realize that *God* is very assertive. His will is going to be accomplished in all things.

The meek Christian has the assurance of a secure future in heaven forever. He also has the assurance that God's desires are being carried out today. The believer does not need to push for results by being self-serving. It is not necessary to take matters into his own hands, conniving and plotting. Planning and hard work are important godly characteristics for the believer. However, the meek believer is able to live in the security of the sovereign will of his Gracious God. Gentleness and meekness are not characteristics of weakness. They are strong characteristics of faith and trust in God. God has all things under control and the believer is a part of that plan. The characteristics of meekness and gentleness are caused by trusting God. They are not entered into by the works of the believer.

God's gentle, meek people are the ones who believe in inheritance by the grace of God (Matthew 5:5 -- "Blessed are the gentle, for they shall inherit the earth").

Christians do not work for their salvation (forgiveness and deliverance from sin). Neither do Christians work for their inheritance (eternity with God). An inheritance is not earned. It is given to children based upon their relationship to the family. Those who are God's children are so called by the grace of God. It is also true that the future inheritance of each believer is securely in place. It is in this graciousness by which the believer is called to live. A life of gentleness and meekness is the fruit that expresses faith in the Sovereign God of grace.

Self Control

When someone is said to be insecure, it usually implies that they are out of control in various areas of their lives. They respond in emotional ways, without stability. This uncontrolled behavior is a reaction to the lack of a secure foundation for their lives. Telling people who are out of control to "grow up" does not solve their problem. Outward changes may even further the difficulties they are already experiencing. The problem: they have taken control of their own lives. They have weakened themselves with the fleshly sins of pride, vanity, fear, and dishonesty. They need to trust the Lord and allow Him to give them the security they need to build upon. Self control can be experienced only as one is under the leadership (control) of the Lord. Once again, if a believer is not secure in the Lord, it will be difficult for him to take his hands off the controls of his life. Self control is jeopardized as well as other aspects of spiritual fruit.

Summary

The spiritual fruit of Galatians 5:22,23 is hindered from growing in the lives of insecure Christians. At times, it may appear that spiritual fruit is completely absent in believers. Why would this be true? Fruitfulness is caused by the nourishment of the soul by the power of the Word of God.

Galatians 5:19-21 speaks of the works of the flesh. These works are the products of insecurity. Insecurity spawns a path of faithlessness which will not allow Christ to grow spiritual fruit in Christians' lives. If Christ is not trusted, mankind is left to his own fleshly works.

Fruit is readily produced by God in the lives of believers who are trusting Christ day by day. The experience of security is heightened when believers are rooted and established in the faith. They have no need to be working for their salvation. They are trusting the Lord completely for this.

Other aspects of fruitfulness are also affected by a person's security in the Lord. Witnessing, wisdom, hospitality, etc., are affected by security or the lack of security in the Lord. The foundation of the matter is this: One cannot live for the Lord without really trusting Him. Genuine trust leads to security. The fruit of the Holy Spirit is produced in secure Christians as they trust the Lord.

Chapter 10

<u>Security and Grace</u>

Oh, the freedom we have each day, walking with God's Son!
No worry, no judgment, no fear -- by faith the victory's won.
For upon the cross, we to the condemning law have died.
And in Christ we live in grace, for in our hearts He does abide.

Security is experienced by the believer only by the grace of God. How then does one acquire the grace of God? God's grace is given to those who humbly seek Him. While, on the other hand, proud people are in opposition to God (James 4:6). Those who live in pride may feel that they have certain qualities or works which elevate their status before God. If one believes that he is "OK" in his own eyes, he may feel that he has no need to cry out to the Lord for help.

Humble people realize their own needs, and as a result, are constantly calling upon the name of the Lord. The sovereign, gracious, almighty God is merciful and kind. He desires to help all those who seek Him and call upon His name.

It is not possible for us to acquire the grace of God by our works. Our "good deeds" are looked upon by the Lord as filthy garments (Isaiah 64:6). If we are proud of these good works, we will trust in them for our salvation and security. When we realize how needy we truly are, we can place ourselves as beggars before the infinitely gracious God. He promises to give grace to us as we seek Him in humility. Then, we can experience the security that *He* gives, rather than a false security of our own making.

Grace can be replaced by legalism (a system of teachings defined below). Legalism focuses on the works of man as meriting some kind of divine favor. When people believe that God's favor is obtained by their own works, faith in God is no longer perceived as necessary. Grace and legalism are in opposition to one another.

Legalism is evident when a person believes that his own works make him acceptable to God or maintain his acceptance before God. The following is a small partial list of works that may be perceived as the cause of spirituality: tithing, visitation, door knocking, witnessing, keeping the Old Testament dietary laws, reading the Bible, attending church services, keeping the ten commandments, being baptized, keeping the rite of circumcision, and showing kindness. "Doing" is the chief characteristic of legalism. However, while the "doing" may be considered to be good, it is not the same as trusting.

The good deeds listed in the preceding paragraph need to be kept in proper perspective. Good deeds are the products of the work of God's grace and faith in the lives of God's children. Man's good deeds can never bring God's grace and faith upon himself.

Legalism is not born from love and security. Legalism is based upon how people see their own works apart from the teachings of the grace of God. It is filled with rules, standing apart from God's grace.

The Old Testament law teaches people to *do* things. Grace teaches people to *receive* things. Only those who perceive themselves to be needy (humble) will turn to God to receive His wondrous grace. If one is a doer, he may not be a recipient of the grace of God. However, it is better to *receive* the grace of God, and *then* by faith to obey the Lord.

The teaching of legalism can cause confusion. The Old Testament law of God is good and perfect. When this good and perfect standard is promoted, people do not want to argue against it. And, indeed they should not! However, acts of keeping God's laws are still deeds, as opposed to faithfully trusting the Lord Jesus Christ.

Because the word of God is perfect, it can never be kept by imperfect man. Man is told to accomplish something that He cannot possibly accomplish. While keeping God's commands, he may fool himself into thinking that his acts of obedience are accepted by God. Some may even say, "If you *do* this, you are not saved," or, "Saved people do not *do* such things!" Clearly, legalists perceive that the emphasis is upon *doing* for the Lord (or for self), rather than *trusting* in the Lord.

The Matter of Faith

Faith is always the work of the Holy Spirit. It is never the work of man. It is a gift from God (Ephesians 2:8). Romans 14:23 tells us that "...whatever is not from faith is sin." Hebrews 11:6 also tells us that without faith it is not possible to please the Lord. Acceptable obedience before the Lord has always been a product of faith. God accepts obedience when the obedience is caused by faith. Obedience does not *produce* faith. However, genuine faith will produce obedience.

Let's get practical. The biblical concept of how faith produces works is not difficult to understand. Faith, grace, and the Holy Spirit are elements of spirituality. These three elements of spirituality are never produced in people by their works. The works of the flesh never have, nor will they ever, make people spiritual. Below are some practical examples:

Why does a Christian *not* read his Bible? He may not read it because at that particular time he does not *believe* it is profitable. He may not *believe* that he needs to read his Bible. His actions are governed by his faith, or his lack of faith.

Why would a believer choose *not* to witness? He may not *believe* that God is with Him at that time. He may not *believe* that God will use the Scriptures as He promised. Once again, activity, or lack thereof, is governed by faith, or the lack of faith.

Why does a Christian refuse baptism? He may not *believe* that it is profitable to be identified with Christ and other believers. He may have a fear of water and therefore does not *believe* that God will protect him in the baptistry. He may not *believe* that baptism is an important step of loving obedience toward the Lord. Faith is still the issue.

Why would a Christian *not* confess his sins to God? He may not *believe* that what he has done is a sin. He may not *believe* that God is gracious enough to forgive him.

Note that in each of the above examples, the lack of good works is a manifestation of a lack of faith. The converse is also true. If a person *believes* that it is profitable to seek and obey the Lord, he will perform good works because of his faith.

Faith was never the work of man at salvation.

(Ephesians 2:8-10). Faith is the *gift* from God. It is not the work of man after salvation. Becoming a child of God has nothing to do with how much or how little of God's commandments a person has kept or has not kept. Becoming a spiritual Christian is not based upon works, either. It is based upon *walking by faith*. We can only avail ourselves as beggars before the grace of God. In humility we can trust Him to mature us each day in Christ. Read Galatians 3:1-3 carefully.

"You foolish Galatians, who has bewitched you, before whose eyes Jesus Christ was publicly portrayed as crucified? This is the only thing I want to find out from you: did you receive the Spirit by the works of the Law, or by hearing with faith? Are you so foolish? Having begun by the Spirit, are you now being perfected by the flesh?"

Faith in God can never be used as a license to sin. One may say, "If this is true, then, I don't have to do anything. I can live my life any way I choose." *The true sequence that God is always pleased with is faith first, and then obedience as a result of that faith (Ephesians 2:8-10; Titus 2:11-14).* It is never works first, and then faith. Truly, it is never faith first, followed by disobedience!

A legalistic Christian accuses God of changing this sequence after a person receives Christ as his Savior. On one hand, he may believe that he is saved by grace through faith. On the other hand, he may believe that his growth in Christian maturity is entirely according to his own works.

A person is saved by grace through faith, and then his obedience proceeds from that faith. This is called "walking by faith" (Colossians 2:6). The purpose of one's faith is to bring forth obedience to the Lord. At times the Christian gets so deeply involved in his activities, that the doing becomes his primary goal.

The primary goal for the believer should never change. He is to always walk by faith. Any lesser goal will eventually end up in a legalistic lifestyle. Such a lifestyle will cause the focus of attentions to be placed upon the weak foundation of man's works. End result: insecurity.

A believer's walk of faith may deteriorate because of an improper view of the grace of God. Another reason may be the pride of talents and gifts given by the Lord for Christian service. A "look what I have done" mentality can arise and ambush a person so that faith is not his motivating factor. The preaching of grace, no matter how forceful it is, can be confused by the loud clanging of fleshly activity.

The Law of God

Erroneous views of God's law may cause a lack of understanding and acceptance of God's grace as a way of life. The Law of God (Old Testament) is a standard by which people are measured. Galatians 3:24,25 says: "Therefore the Law has become our tutor to lead us to Christ, that we may be justified by faith. But now that faith has come, we are no longer under a tutor." The law continues to lead us to Christ after we are saved. The perfect law will always show our need for forgiveness and the need for the grace of God in our lives.

After a person has received Christ, the standard for living is no longer law, but Christ (Grace). The Lord Jesus Christ is now the Divine Measuring Rod for the believer. Following Christ does not leave the believer without biblical standards. On the contrary, this Standard (Christ) is even more comprehensive than the Old Testament Law. Now, *everything* that the believer does is brought to Christ for His divine approval.

The Christian no longer has ten commandments to follow, but rather, the Lord Jesus Christ Himself. Lying, cheating, stealing, adultery, murder, etc., are all disapproved by Christ. However, the believer has an entire life to submit before God in Christ.

Therefore, Christ is the only standard that brings completeness (maturity) to the Christian. The act of keeping individual Old Testament laws or groups of them never affects the believer's life with completeness. Only a day by day walk of faith with the Lord Jesus Christ can accomplish the scriptural goal of spiritual maturity.

The Old Testament Law and the Teachings of Christ

Understanding the place of the Old Testament law may be confusing. Christ quoted from the Old Testament, even from the ten commandments. Some may believe that the Old Testament Law is to be followed as a part of Christ's teachings. To these, the Old Testament remains as a standard for the believer to follow in order to become spiritual. The answers to this statement are as follows:

Having Christ as Savior does not nullify the intent of the Old Testament Law. God's perfect law does not go away. The intent of the law is to bring people to Christ. The intent of the Law to Israel was the same. It was intended to bring them to the altar of sacrifice. It was there at the altar that they were manifesting their faith in God's gracious forgiveness. Keeping the Old Testament law was never an end in itself. The intended purpose was to cause people to see how needy they really were. When they saw the truth of what they were like, they would humbly go to the altar, call upon the Lord, and worship Him.

When a believer in Christ sins, he acts like an unsaved person; he is acting outside the realm of grace, apart from Christ. The Word of God brings conviction, guilt, and condemnation. Christ, the Advocate, intercedes for him and sets him free (I John 2:1). Through this process the Christian needs to see himself as he truly is, a needy soul before the Lord. The humble believer turns to Christ for forgiveness and cleansing (I John 1:9). Thus, God's Word has the same affect, to bring the believer back to Christ.

The Gospels of Matthew, Mark, Luke, and John were written from the Old Testament dispensation of the Law. Christ had not yet died, neither had He been raised from the dead, nor had the church been established. Thus, the Four Gospels were given under the dispensation of the Old Testament Law.

The four Gospels provide a transition between dispensations. The dispensation of God's dealing with Israel is separated from the dispensation of God's dealings with the church. The dispensation of this present age began after the ascension of Christ, on the Day of Pentecost (Acts 2). The quotations in the Gospels from the ten commandments by Christ are still dealing with the Old Testament dispensation. The purpose of the law in the Gospels was still the same -- to bring people to the place of worshipping God.

Christ defining the heart of the Old Testament.

Under the law of Moses, no one would have been stoned for thinking adulterous thoughts or harboring hatred in his heart for his brother. Christ taught that such a person was as guilty as the one who practiced the outward acts of adultery and murder (Matthew 5).

The Old Testament law was given to show all people to be defective. Today, man stands condemned even in his thoughts. Christ was showing the need in the heart of man. Helpless before God, mankind needs forgiveness and cleansing. The Law of God could never cleanse. It could only condemn.

The Old Testament Law and Security

If keeping just one portion of the Old Testament Law would make God pleased with the Christian, then, the Christian is no longer secure. The same doubts and fears that are raised regarding the eternal security of the believer are raised here. No one can perfectly keep the Law of God. Since God's standard is perfection, God would not be pleased with the Christian's deeds no matter how great or perfect those deeds may appear to man.

As an example, let us take just one of the Ten Commandments: honoring parents. A Christian may reason thus: "As a believer in Christ, how do I know when I have honored my parents enough, the way that God wants me to? What if there is a brief portion of time that I fail to honor them? What if I do not honor them perfectly? God's standard in this commandment is perfection. I have not perfectly kept this command. I am guilty of the whole law of God (James 2:10,11). I have become displeasing to God in my life. I have become guilty!" Result: condemnation and insecurity.

The answer to the above dilemma is this: "I will honor my parents because I believe that God wants me to honor them. I will honor them not because I am being forced to honor them. As I obey the Lord in this command, He will accept my work as perfect. He will accept this obedience because I have obeyed God's Word by faith. I have obeyed by faith to please Him."

God accepts the believers works as perfect when those works are done by faith in Him. The answer to the problem is not "how much" nor "how," but "why." In this sense, the reason behind obedience is more important than the obedience. Dead works (works practiced outside of faith in God) are never acceptable to God (Hebrews 11:6). This is true whether dead works are practiced by believers or unbelievers.

Thus, if believers are counting on their works done apart from faith to please God, they will always remain insecure. They could not live up to God's perfection before they became Christians. They cannot live up to God's perfect standards after they become Christians. However, God does accept their works as perfect if they are done out of the motivation of faith in God and His word.

"Good Enough" vs. Perfection

The argument that legalists give at this point is: "God understands. He knows people's weaknesses and overlooks their failings. As long as people do the best that they can, God knows the heart." In other words, they say that God overlooks imperfections and excuses sins. This is not true. Exodus 34:7 says, "...He will by no means leave the guilty unpunished."

The standard that people use to calm their fears is

113

the standard called "Good Enough." This standard is based upon people "doing their best." It is a comparative standard, comparing the activity and acceptance of people. This is unwise.

II Corinthians 10:12 -- "For we are not bold to class or compare ourselves with some of those who commend themselves; but when they measure themselves by themselves, and compare themselves with themselves, they are without understanding."

However, God *does* expect more from people than their best. He expects a perfection that they cannot attain (Matthew 5:48 "Therefore you are to be perfect, as your heavenly Father is perfect"). To legalists this command only applies to those who are unsaved. Selective obedience and application of the Scriptures will not cause security with God. No one is exempt from His perfect standards.

Selective obedience is characteristic of all systems of legalism. The choice of commandments to obey is made on the basis of what is perceived to be pleasing to God. The religious participants are the ones who determine which commandments to obey. Those who are keeping certain commands are considered to be spiritual. The ones who are not keeping certain commands are considered to be carnal, or even lost.

Summary
Security for the believer has always been and always will be based upon what Christ has done and Who He is. It is *not* based upon who man is and what man does. This fact does not change after a person receives Christ by grace through faith. The secure rock

of faith is the same at the time of a person's salvation as well as after he is saved.

The perfection that God sees in the believer as he lives is the same perfection He sees in the believer at the time of his salvation. This perfection is Jesus Christ. Taking this perfection away is the same as taking Christ away from the believer. As discussed in Chapter 3, this cannot happen.

Therefore, legalists are not only insecure, but they are also promoters of insecurity regarding their views of law-keeping. They never know how much of the law kept will please God. They teach others to be just "good enough." They compare themselves with others in order to claim spirituality. All these attempts are built upon the insecure foundations of man's ideas, standards, and works.

Security for the believer is based upon the grace of God. It is not founded upon the weakness of the fleshly works of mankind.

Chapter 11

The Judgment Seat of Christ
(A "No-Win" Scenario for Legalism)

The joy of His presence finally to set us free,
The grace of God poured out for you and me,
Standing before Him with no more sin at last,
For the flesh and its lusts are all in the past.

II Corinthians 5:10 -- "For we must all appear before the judgment seat of Christ, that each one may be recompensed for his deeds in the body, according to what he has done, whether good or bad."

One of the most popular tools of legalism promoting insecurity in Christianity is a flawed view of the judgment seat of Christ. Christian legalists enjoy threatening other Christians by saying that all Christians will give an account of themselves before this judgment seat. This is a true statement (see verse above). The usage of the words "terror, loss, sadness, regret, etc.," is common when preaching and writing on this topic. Even when trying to assure people that it won't be *too* bad, just as long as they "do their best," the approach can still be legalistic.

Trying to get people to live for the Lord is a noble endeavor. However, using the unscriptural motivation of

116

fear to accomplish this goal is wrong.

Has every Christian "done their best?" What if Christians do not confess all of their sins? What if all their sins are not confessed *perfectly?* What if they overlooked some "insignificant" sins? Christ's standard has not changed. It is still perfection. Legalism puts every Christian in a hopeless situation before the judgment seat of Christ. There is no way he or she could possibly live up to the perfect expectations of God at the judgment seat.

This judgment is for the believer's works. What if the Christian has not always worked hard enough or long enough? What if he has served the Lord only occasionally or with improper motives in mind? The same insecure view regarding salvation is promoted by legalists for the working Christian. There is no possible way a Christian can be secure in Christ while he is standing in fear of judgment. Under the realm of legalism, believers are never perfect before God. Their best efforts are always tainted with self and sin.

The Greek judgment seat was a place of reward for athletes who had competed in various events. Only the athletes who won would be standing before the judgment seat. Therefore, the purpose was to reward, not to condemn. None of the athletes standing before the reward platform would be made to feel terror or regret. The purpose was not to cause the athletes to feel guilty or fearful.

The Christian is the winner. Each believer (winner) will be standing before the judgment seat of Christ. Unbelievers are the losers. They will not be present at the judgment seat of Christ. Their judgment is future, at the great white throne judgment (Revelation 20:11-15).

These might be the words of the judge as interpreted by the legalists: "Here's your reward for winning. Even though you did an imperfect job, you still get this reward because you were good enough. However, you should have lifted your knees higher and you should have pumped your arms faster. You should have chosen better running shoes. Please stand to the right while I burn up your worthless works. By the way, welcome to heaven." This is a representation of the common, but utterly flawed view of many legalists at the judgment seat of Christ.

Purgatory

The doctrine of purgatory may be unknowingly taught by some legalist believers. They teach Revelation 21:4 to mean that God will wipe away all tear from the eyes of *all* church saints. The timing of this event occurs after the millennium.

Many Christians have died between the time of Christ's ascension to the present. Their spirits have gone home to be with the Lord. Since this is the case, they are all waiting in fear of this "purgatory," the burning away of their worthless deeds. One thousand years is a long time to be experiencing regret and tears in the presence of the Bridegroom. Not even on this sin-cursed planet did Jesus allow his disciples to manifest such sadness (Matthew 9:15). Yet, the legalist views the believer standing before Christ in heaven in great sadness and regret. What a strange marriage!

For some unanswerable reason, the legalist perceives that God will not see the believer's works through the veil of Christ's perfection at the judgment seat. The Christian legalist has a God who changes. His God sees the believer as perfect in Christ while the believer remains on earth. In heaven, the legalist has a God Who takes away the perfection of Christ. Under this view, *all* believers' works are tinder, because none of them are perfect. If the perfection of Christ is taken away from the believer at any time, he becomes the object of the wrath of God.

II Corinthians 5:11 -- "Therefore knowing the fear of the Lord, we persuade men, but we are made manifest to God; and I hope that we are made manifest also in your consciences."

The above verse has often been used to back up the legalistic view of the judgment seat of Christ. In actuality, it is the *beginning* of a section on witnessing, reconciliation, and ambassadorship for Christ. God is not a terror to the believer, but to the lost. This subject has been covered in Chapter 7. The Christian is at peace with God. He is a friend of the Lord Jesus Christ.

The legalistic view of the judgment seat of Christ opposes the theology of the rapture and of heaven. The theology of I John 3:1-3 tells us that there will be a radical change in all believers when they stand before the Lord. When does this change occur? Does it occur before or after the Judgment Seat of Christ? It is plainly taught that the home going of the church of God will take place before the judgment of the believer's works.

"See how great a love the Father has bestowed upon us, that we should be called children of God; and such we are. For this reason the world does not know us, because it did not know Him. Beloved, now we are children of God, and it has not appeared as yet what we shall be.   We know that, when He appears, we

shall be like Him, because we shall see Him just as He is. And everyone who has this hope fixed on Him purifies himself, just as He is pure." I John 3:1-3

When Christ appears (the rapture of the church), the believer is going to go home to be with the Lord. When this occurs, he will be given a new body. The believer's new heavenly body will not be a body controlled by fleshly desires. His new body will be like Christ's glorified body. Christ's body was not, is not, and will not be controlled nor motivated by sinful fleshly desires.

This change will occur (verse 2) *before* the event of the judgment of the believers' works. First Corinthians 15:51,52 also tells of this great transition for the believer:

"Behold, I tell you a mystery; we shall not all sleep, but we shall all be changed, in a moment, in the twinkling of an eye, at the last trumpet; for the trumpet will sound, and the dead will be raised imperishable, and we shall be changed."

The changing of the believer will take place "in the twinkling of an eye." No longer will he enjoy sin. He will despise it. He will no longer have the body of fleshly lusts. God "will transform the body of our humble state into conformity with the body of His glory, by the exertion of the power that He has even to subject all things to Himself." Philippians 3:21.

Because of this radical change in the believer, the Christian will rejoice with Christ at the burning up of all his worthless works. He will not be disappointed. He will be glad. The legalistic view puts the Christian in heaven with his old fleshly desires. The Bible puts the believer in heaven with his new spiritual Christ-like desires. While Christians may presently see heaven through eyes of flesh, they will see it differently when they get there. They will be like Jesus. Therefore, they will see their worthless deeds as Jesus does.

The loss of the worthless deeds of the believer at the judgment seat of Christ will be a time of great blessing. Fleshly loss and spiritual gain have always been a benefit and a source of rejoicing for the believer in Christ. Every time a Christian is stripped his own worthless works for the sake of Christ, he is blessed by God. Philippians 3:3-8 speaks of the blessing Paul acknowledges while losing fleshly attainments for the sake of Christ:

"But whatever things were gain to me, those things I have counted as loss for the sake of Christ. More than that, I count all things to be loss in view of the surpassing value of knowing Christ Jesus my Lord, for whom I have suffered the loss of all things, and count them but rubbish in order that I may gain Christ."

Paul knew that the works of the flesh were obstacles standing in the path of God's grace through the Lord Jesus Christ. The judgment seat of Christ will be the grand finale. The loss of these deeds (rubbish) and the gaining of Christ is to be looked forward to by every Christian.

Sin and the Judgment Seat

We are taught in I Corinthians 3 that the judgment seat of Christ will be a judgment of the believer's works, not the believer's sins. The believer's sins have already been judged at the cross of Calvary. Jesus' blood has washed them all away forever. This includes all the believer's past sins, present sins, and any sins that he would commit in the future.

However, there remains a direct correlation between sin and works. When a Christian commits sin, his works are going to be affected. He will be driven by wrong motives. He will be operating in the flesh, carnal. He will become lazy toward the Lord. The only way a Christian will have works that are rubbish is when he allows unconfessed sin to remain in his life. When all sin has been confessed, the believer will be walking in the righteousness of the Lord. The point is: sin causes worthless works and righteousness (Christ's) causes acceptable rewardable works.

If the believer is living in the righteousness of Christ, he will be producing gold, silver, and precious stones. If he is living in sin, he will be producing wood, hay, and stubble. Worthless deeds at the judgment seat of Christ will remind the Christian of his sins. Worthless deeds will remind him of his weaknesses, failures, and pride. When these deeds are purged (burnt up), it is difficult to imagine any Christian feeling sorrow or regret at the loss of these fleshly expressions.

I can personally testify of the failures caused by my sins and by the weaknesses of my flesh. I am greatly saddened by the remembrance of the worthless deeds that I have done. I am even more grieved by remembering the cause (sin) of those worthless deeds. I remember selfish motives and improper behavior. I remember the lack of doing my best for the Lord. I am looking forward to the judgment seat of Christ. The remembrance of my failures will all be burnt up at that time. May God be praised!

Proper Motivation for Service

Grace is God's love in motion, seeking to bring about all that He has providentially determined. In His graciousness, God has determined to bring Himself to man. The true Christian is the only person who has a Seeking God Who is interested in finding and reviving lost sinners.

Grace is the unmerited favor of God upon man, whereby God has chosen to pour out His goodness upon man. Grace is a great force in the life of the believer. God has obligated Himself to mankind. To ignore God's graciousness is the ultimate of all sin. However, receiving this grace gives man an obligation. This is a moral obligation. First John 2:6 says, "The one who says he abides in Him ought himself to walk in the same manner as He walked."

Grace has been improperly defined by some, causing people to think that God excuses sin. Grace is not leniency nor indulgence. It is not an act of ignoring sin.

Luke 7:36-47 tells the story of proper motivation for serving the Lord. It tells how love and grace obligate believers to serve Christ.

Jesus Christ was invited to dinner by a Pharisee. While He was there, a woman of ill repute used a vial of precious perfume to anoint Christ's feet. She then continued to wash His feet with her tears and dry them with her hair. The Pharisees were offended at the presence of this woman. They wondered why Christ was not offended. It was then that Christ told the story of how love and forgiveness had obligated this woman to show love and service to Him. In verses 44-47, Jesus spoke to Simon, the Pharisee, and said:

"I entered your house; you gave Me no water for My feet, but she has wet My feet with her tears, and wiped them with her hair. You gave Me no kiss; but she, since the time I came in, has not ceased to kiss My feet. You did not anoint My head with oil, but she anointed My feet with perfume. For this reason I say to you, her sins, which are many, have been forgiven, for she loved much; but he who is forgiven little, loves little."

The Pharisees did not think they needed Christ's love. They did not think that they had a debt to be forgiven. Therefore, in their minds, they were not under any obligation to Christ. They did not feel that they were obligated to provide a simple basin of water for the tired dusty feet of the Savior. They were "good enough."

This is an unfortunate, yet common outlook of many people today. It is prevalent among unbelievers as well as believers. In this way, legalism fools people into thinking that they do not need much forgiveness. Therefore, they feel that they do not owe much to God.

Christ's love propels us into service and obedience for Him. We have been loved much. In the truest sense, we have been and are loved infinitely. Therefore, we owe an infinite amount of love to God in return.

Legalists use the judgment seat of Christ as a club to bully Christians into submission and obedience. When I spoke to a Christian lady about this, she asked, "Then what keeps us serving the Lord? What keeps us obedient? What stops us from going astray?"

If I meditate upon the grace and love of God in Christ for me, I will be a better Christian servant than if I fear retribution at the Judgment Seat of Christ. God's graciousness and forgiveness to me have been great. So great, that it controls my life when I dwell on it. If I do not think upon the great grace and great love of God for me, I will go astray. Second Corinthians 5:14 says, "For the love of Christ controls us." It is not God's law of the judgment seat of Christ that controls us. It is His love that controls us.

If we are motivated by the love of God, we are motivated properly. Obeying God because we love Him is acceptable to Him (John 14:15; II Corinthians 5:14). If we are motivated by the fear of loss of rewards, we are motivated improperly.

Obedience which is motivated out of fear is selfishness. Such obedience is done so that *we* will not suffer loss or lose rewards. When the judgment seat of Christ is used to cause fear, love is no longer the motivating factor. All works done out of fear of losing rewards will be loss at the judgment seat of Christ. Why? Because they were done for self and not for Christ.

One of the arguments of the legalist regarding the judgment seat is that our deeds must be done with the proper motivation. This is true. First Corinthians 10:31 tells us that everything we do is to be done to the glory of God. If our lives are motivated out of fear of loss of rewards, the motivation is not the glory of God. The motivation becomes the glory of self. Fear motivates people so that *they* will not lose rewards.

We claim that God loves us with an everlasting love (Jeremiah 31:3). It may surprise the reader that we do not want God to love us. If we take more love than we think we deserve, we will have too great of an obligation. We might feel as though we have to faithfully love Him in return. It is very clear from the teachings of Christ that love and obedience go together. In John 14:15, Jesus said, "If you love Me, you will keep My commandments." The basic motivating question is not whether or not we are obedient. Rather, it is whether or not we really love the Lord.

Summary

The one who has the hope of being with Christ will be purifying his life to be like Christ (I John 3:3). The one who has received grace will live in that grace. The security of heaven has a direct result upon the lifestyle of the believer. As previously discussed, eternity can only be entered into by grace through faith.

The believer is secure in heaven, not because of his works, but because of the grace of God. So also, the believer is secure in works that please God, not because of his own strength, but because of the grace of God. Joyful security is based upon the anticipation of glory, not the anticipation of judgment.

Fear of judgment is to be replaced by receiving God's love and living in that love. God's graciousness causes us to respond to Him in love. We are thus compelled to obey Him.

Chapter 12

Trials: Blessings or Curses?

The depths of despair so low, trials and tests abounding in life,
Sickness, sorrow and afflictions increase, with hatred and its strife.
Is God so cruel and so feeble that He cannot take away the toils of man?
Isn't there more to His awesome ways as He unfolds His wondrous plan?

The Rock of Gibraltar stands as a mountain of security, towering over the ocean. For thousands of years storms have pounded this awesome creation. To no avail, it continues to stand as a testimony of the strength of its Creator.

So also is the believer who is secure in the Lord Jesus Christ. When the storms of trials and tests cast their strength against the Christian, it only enhances the power of the Creator and Sustainer of life. It may sound strange, but when Christians realize their weaknesses, God's strength can then be shown to the trusting believer.

The God of the Bible is looked upon in one of two ways: either He is a God of unfairness and cruelty, or He is a God of justice and love. In Genesis 4, Cain viewed God as unfair. He retaliated by murdering his own brother. Abel, on the other hand, saw God as loving and kind. He humbly offered an acceptable sacrifice to God. He believed that God would accept that which was not the work of his own hands. This seemed greatly unfair to Cain, who worked and labored to bring his *own* fruit in his *own* way to the Lord as a sacrifice.

God must have appeared to be extremely unfair to all those who died in the flood as Noah escaped unscathed. Inside the ark, Noah and his family were safe and secure in the love of God.

Trials and tests in the believer's life can be handled in one of two ways: with rebellion ("God is unfair.") or with acceptance ("God loves me and is teaching me."). However, the fleshly mind of the unbeliever has no choice but to react adversely when trials come his way.

The Bible also cautions that the believer can develop ungodly attitudes during trials. People, events, and varying situations can be looked upon as a source of bitterness (Ephesians 4:31). Those who do not hold to the security of the believer have no recourse, no defense. They must doubt God's love when trials and tests come into their lives. They have no option but to feel that God is angry with them. They must believe that God is punishing them for something they did that was wrong, or something that they did not complete.

On the other hand, the one holding to the security of the believer is able to trust the Lord. He is able to go through uncomfortable and devastating circumstances while recognizing God's love.

Trials and tests are allowed into believers' lives to fulfill God's purposes. These purposes are all for the honor and glory of the Lord. The purposes of God in allowing difficulties into our lives may be placed into four categories: discipline, trust, worship, and hope.

Discipline

Have you ever been in a quiet restaurant enjoying a meal, while undisciplined children were allowed to misbehave at the next table? Tempers flaring, children crying, and confusion all take away from a peaceful, pleasant atmosphere. As you observe the situation, you conclude, "These parents really don't love their kids." The children exemplify the same selfishness that their parents possess.

Discipline is the chief goal for trials and tests in the believer as mentioned in Hebrews 12:5-8:

" **And you have forgotten the exhortation which is addressed to you as sons, 'My son, do not regard lightly the discipline of the Lord, Nor faint when you are reproved by Him; For those whom the Lord loves He disciplines, And He scourges every son whom He receives.' It is for discipline that you endure; God deals with you as with sons; for what son is there whom his father does not discipline? But if you are without discipline, of which all have become partakers, then you are illegitimate children and not sons.**"

God loves His children, and because He loves them, He disciplines them. He brings or allows unpleasant circumstances of varying degrees into the lives of His children. These trials are intended to cause God's children to change for the better.

The word "discipline" means to punish by whipping. This indeed, is an extreme measure employed to change behavior, especially in our present lenient society. Whipping is surely a harsh form of punishment. However, the purpose is certain to get the attention of the one being flogged. *God wants to get the attention of His people.*

The Lord desires to produce endurance (patience) in His children's lives. An undisciplined Christian is a contradiction in terms. Note that the basis of these chastisements is sonship, being securely related to God. Discipline is an outward proof that the believer belongs to God. If the believer did not belong to God, no discipline would be necessary. Discipline is the proof that God loves His children. Endurance (patience) is the fruit the Lord desires to produce in His children's lives. Without discipline, the believer becomes like those undisciplined "spoiled brats" in the restaurant.

Trust

The believer has many weaknesses. It is good for the Christian to recognize his own faltering fleshly nature. God allows trials and tests into a believer's life to accentuate the inabilities of man. Only one choice is left for God's children. The believer *must* look upward. Looking inward (toward his weak flesh) will not give him the necessary strength through times of trials. The Christian will find only continued failures and weaknesses within himself.

The Lord knows the Christian's weaknesses and causes him to face circumstances that are completely out of his control. Repeated lessons throughout life are necessary for the Christian. The constant knowledge of the weakness of the flesh drives believers to the One in Whom they *can* trust, the Lord Jesus Christ.

An interesting point: we fail to realize that all circumstances are already out of our control. Most of us need to be reminded of it. God uses trials to accomplish this.

II Corinthians 12:7-10 -- "And because of the

surpassing greatness of the revelations, for this reason, to keep me from exalting myself, there was given me a thorn in the flesh, a messenger of Satan to buffet me-- to keep me from exalting myself! Concerning this I entreated the Lord three times that it might depart from me. And He has said to me, 'My grace is sufficient for you, for power is perfected in weakness.' Most gladly, therefore, I will rather boast about my weaknesses, that the power of Christ may dwell in me. Therefore I am well content with weaknesses, with insults, with distresses, with persecutions, with difficulties, for Christ's sake; for when I am weak, then I am strong."

Trusting God is the strongest position a believer can attain. When one is truly trusting the Lord, he stops trusting in himself. It is then that the power of God is made known to the Christian. Then, and only then, can one have the victory of the Lord in his life. God enables the believer with *His* strength. As a result, the believer can confidently walk with the Lord, to do God's will by faith. This pleases the Lord.

The Lord knows best. He knows that the arm of man's flesh is weak. God also knows that His own arm is strong. He knows that the arm of the flesh cannot bring a person to the strength only found in trusting Him. Only faith in God can allow the believer to experience the work of God in his life. Trials are meant to increase a believer's faith in God.

Worship

Worship is one of the results that God intends to bring into the lives of His people as they are put through trials and tests. When Christians go through trials, there are times that they are made aware that the only thing they can do is worship. They can only sit before the throne of God and tell Him, "I don't know what you are teaching me. I don't have any answers for these problems. But I do know that You have my full attention."

Worship occurs when God has our full submissive attention. It is at times of great affliction that we recognize anew that God is the potter and we are the clay in His hands. Isaiah 64:8 shows God's pleasure in those who worship Him with this submissiveness: "But now, O Lord, Thou art our Father, We are the clay, and Thou our potter; And all of us are the work of Thy hand."

This is an interesting position of security for the believer. We are dirt (clay). Recognition of our position before our Creator places us in the most secure place of all -- in the Potter's hands. This is most humbling. It is also the highest form of worship that we can attain. Trials and tests cause us to be humbled to the place where we truly seek to ascribe worth to God.

God's will is for His people to be brought back into that right relationship of security, fellowship, and worship. Often, the believer waits for the trial to pass before he worships the Lord. This is a mistake. Bowing before the Lord in submission to testing is an act of worship. It shows confidence in God. Rebellion in times of trials bypasses God's intent to bring the believer to worship.

Hope

Romans 5:3 -- "And not only this, but we also exult in our tribulations, knowing that tribulation brings about perseverance; and perseverance, proven

character; and proven character, hope; and hope does not disappoint, because the love of God has been poured out within our hearts through the Holy Spirit who was given to us."

Our lack of control over our lives and over the world provides unending examples of our inabilities. Trials and tests have a way of illustrating constant weaknesses. We are hopeless! Trials and tests merely bring the truth of hopelessness to the surface. To ignore the truth of our hopelessness is a serious mistake.

Death is the ultimate demonstration of the inabilities of mankind. Trials and tests have a way of teaching us how weak and hopeless we really are. The process that takes us there is certain. Many trials along the way remind us that we can do nothing except to look to Him Who is in control of all things. Jesus Christ alone is our secure hope. This is the only way we can properly survive in this sin-cursed world, with all of its disease, sorrow, and death.

Some have been alarmed at the climbing suicide rate. Frankly, I am not alarmed. Without the Lord Jesus Christ, people have no anticipation for eternity. They have no hope. However, believers have great anticipation for the future. If people do not have a secure hope for the future, then they are of all men "most miserable" (I Corinthians 15:19 -- KJV).

II Corinthians 4:16-18 -- "Therefore we do not lose heart, but though our outer man is decaying, yet our inner man is being renewed day by day. For momentary, light affliction is producing for us an eternal weight of glory far beyond all comparison, while we look not at the things which are seen,   but

at the things which are not seen; for the things which are seen are temporal, but the things which are not seen are eternal."

Trials and tests cause us to focus our attentions upon the things that really matter. We are forced to rely upon our only Secure and True Hope, the Lord Jesus Christ. While trusting in Christ, the believer can positively anticipate the future. Without trials and tests, it is easy to place our concerns upon temporary earthly things. God uses our weaknesses and deterioration of life to point us to our Eternal Rock. There is and never will be another hope.

Summary

Discipline, trust, worship, and hope are God's intended results for the believer as he goes through trials and tests. Improper responses would be rebellion, doubt, idolatry (covetousness), and despair. The first set of purposes is from the Lord. The second set of responses is from the fleshly lusts of man's heart.

Once again, the truths concerning the character of the love of God will form our relationships into secure lifestyles. Do we really believe that God is good to us to allow these unfavorable circumstances into our lives? Or, do we believe that He is cruel, uncaring, and unfair?

God allows trials to come into our lives to develop our submission and trust in Him. Submission and trust bring the blessings of peace and happiness in any and all circumstances. The alternative to this submissive response would be rebellion. The result of rebellion brings the curses of disappointment and bitterness.

Chapter 13

Secure Relationships

Others - others - We're not alone. Our lives are filled with others.
Bosses, friends, husbands, wives - Our sisters and our brothers.
Why are they there? For what purpose are they placed in our road?
Are they present to be a blessing? Or merely to add to our heavy load?

Ephesians 5:18-21 -- "And do not get drunk with wine, for that is dissipation, but be filled with the Spirit, speaking to one another in psalms and hymns and spiritual songs, singing and making melody with your heart to the Lord; always giving thanks for all things in the name of our Lord Jesus Christ to God, even the Father; and be subject to one another in the fear of Christ."

Everyone wants to have secure relationships with people. Often, it is sought after in wrong places. If people look to others for security, they will always be disappointed. Security must first be established by a personal relationship with God through Christ. While pursuing good sound relationships, one must never turn away from the One and Only True Foundation. When one's relationship with God is insecure, so also will be his relationships with people.

135

Unfortunately, security is equated with strong and forceful personalities. People wish they could be more assertive. They wish they could stand up for themselves. They wish they had more courage. They would like to be more threatening and to be feared.

It is common to step on others while standing up for one's own rights. This is biblically and ethically wrong. Aggressiveness does not foster security. It only serves to bring a temporary satisfaction of the flesh. This temporary satisfaction quickly fades. The need to become aggressive soon returns. Other confrontations and victories are sought after and gained. This repetitive process can be followed until all relationships are either dominated or terminated.

If a certain relationship cannot be dominated, it is then perceived as a threat. Unnecessary confrontation and competition can be the results of insecure aggressiveness. Relationships become greatly strained or destroyed. People may be entirely rejected or accepted based upon this false perception of security.

The one who insists on being forceful and dominant may very well be the one who lacks real security. The one who does not need to be the *controller* may be the one who has security. His need for security may have already been met in his life through faith in Christ.

Many marriages are good havens of security, even though both spouses may come from relationships where they are not completely accepted. Their own personal relationships in family, employment, and church may have been intolerable. If the individual marriage partners are secure in the grace of God, their married relationship may be completely secure. While other relationships may have had the aspirations of domineering people attached, the marriage may not.

How does God work secure relationships into the lives of believers? God's Word constantly testifies that He is God. He is to be trusted. He is in control of all things. People are in control of nothing. God is in charge of eternal life. Mankind is not in control of his own destiny. Man is only secure in God. Nothing can separate the believer from God. God is forever the Friend of the Christian. He meets every need that man has. Even the trials and tests experienced by mankind are designed to draw people closer to the Rock of security.

God's plan takes an opposite path from the world's plan. God's plan for security is experienced when people become submissive to His plan. Security from the world's perspective is based upon independence, wealth, health, and domination.

We are not in control of how tall we are, how many hairs grow on our heads, nor how long we will live. *God alone is in control of all things.*

With this arsenal of security, the Christian, and only the Christian, can face life successfully. Listen to the message of "no fear" in these three Bible verses:

Psalm 56:4 -- "In God I will praise his word, in God I have put my trust; I will not fear what flesh can do unto me."

Psalm 118:6 -- "The Lord is on my side; I will not fear: what can man do unto me?"

Hebrews 13:6 -- "So that we may boldly say, The Lord is my helper, and I will not fear what man shall do unto me."

The message in each believer's heart should be: "I am trusting the Lord. The Lord is by my side. The Lord is my helper. What can possibly make me become fearful?"

In practice, the Christian can perform the acts of submission as commanded by Ephesians 5:21. By recognizing that God is in full control of *all* situations, the believer has no need to control others. He is assured that God alone is the only Forceful, Domineering Person in the whole universe.

People may stamp their feet, pout, and scream. They may even become physically abusive to others. People have no foundation upon which they try to usurp the authoritative position held by God alone. God is still in control. He always has been and always will be God. Expressions of enforcing one's ways upon others offer no threat to God's sovereign control. The Christian who is trusting in God has nothing to fear.

The Lord mocks the pitiful efforts of man as he tries to be in control of things:

Psalm 2:1-4 --"Why are the nations in an uproar, And the peoples devising a vain thing? The kings of the earth take their stand, And the rulers take counsel together against the Lord and against His Anointed: 'Let us tear their fetters apart, and cast away their cords from us!' He who sits in the heavens laughs, The Lord scoffs at them."

The trusting believer who is secure in the Lord, is not threatened. He and God are together always. When people become domineering, they compete with God. To be in competition with God will only bring insecurity and defeat into the lives of people. A physical victory may be won only to ultimately experience spiritual defeat.

The Israelites lusted after meat in the wilderness. In their cravings, they demanded their desires to be satisfied. Psalm 106:15 tells us that "he (God) gave them their request; but sent leanness into their soul." (KJV). The lusts of people, ruling over their lives, can drive them to find satisfaction. However, in the process, they may lose what they thought they were gaining. The Israelites thought they were really living. The book of Numbers records their defeat. As they ate the meat they desired, the Lord brought judgment upon them (Numbers 11:31-34).

Three main practical areas of life are affected by one's security or insecurity. A fourth area (The Local Church) will be discussed in the following chapter. The three to be discussed here are family and home, employment, and peer relationships. All other practical areas may fit under these main headings.

Family and Home

It is essential for parents to discipline their children. Those who do not practice discipline are not concerned for their children's welfare and happiness. Discipline is the response of love from parents to their children. It is not cruelty. It is correction. It is not a war to see which party gets their way, children or parents. It is a process to help form children's values and responsibilities.

Insecurity in the lives of parents can damage the purpose of discipline. It may seem to them a matter of competition, rather than instruction. These insecurities can be handed down to their children. A downward spiraling can continue until the Lord interrupts such trends with His gracious hand. As people learn to trust the Lord, the need for them to control people and circumstances diminishes. So also does the need to win "contests" with their children. This cycle of insecurity is broken when faith in God is manifested.

My father was an extremely insecure, domineering parent. The atmosphere of our home was inflamed by alcohol, gambling, sexual abuse, and frequent beatings. Tension was a constant companion. Everyone (except Dad) behaved as if they were walking on eggs, waiting for something or someone to crack. Finally, when I was age twelve, my dad had a "nervous breakdown." He spent many years in and out of a mental hospital. However, the feelings of insecurity, hatred, fear, and cruelty had already been developed in the lives of my brother, my sisters, and me.

At age seventeen, at a Christian camp, I received Jesus Christ as my personal Savior. I received forgiveness of sins and the free gift of eternal life. I knew where I was going if I should die. The war between God and me was over (Romans 5:1). For the first time in my life I had real security and peace. The joy of having sins forgiven and taken away set me free (Psalm 103:12).

God immediately began to build a new life where the old one once was. This new life had the secure foundation of eternity. The insecurities of self-assertion and selfish cruelties soon began to fade. It was not long before the Lord directed me to prepare for the ministry of the gospel. Before graduation from college, I became a pastor. At the time of this writing, I have been a pastor for over twenty-five years. During this time, I have been telling people how to become secure. I came from extreme insecurity to a position where I was teaching others how to be secure. Truly, God's plan is awesome!

This personal illustration reveals how the cycle of insecurity can be broken. We do not have to languish in the depths of our childhood disappointments. *Instead of living a life of blaming others for how we turned out, we have freedom in Christ to change.*

We do not have to become our parents, our spouses, our brother, or our sister. We do not have to become our gang leader, our professor, our boss, our classmate, or our co-worker. We can be free to be the kind of people God wants us to be. Jesus taught us that He came to set us free. He is the truth that brings freedom indeed (John 8:32).

I was visiting a family where husband and wife were having marital difficulties. Both professed to be saved. The woman defended the abusive behavior of her husband. He had been raised in an atmosphere of neglect and abuse. She said, "He has a difficult time showing love, because he was shown no love while he was a child." My response to her was that of my own personal testimony. How can a Christian truthfully testify that he does not know love? That is like saying that a Christian does not know God!

God, our Heavenly Father, has been loving and gracious to us beyond what words can describe. His love is infinite. There is no end to it. There is no limit to His forgiveness and acceptance of us. He not only rescued us, but He cleansed us, and put joy in our hearts. If we are God's children, we know what love is. If we are not saved, we can only guess or wish.

Bitterness is an unfortunate and sinful quality of life. It is enhanced in the lives of those who continue to reflect upon their own difficult and sometimes evil circumstances. Jacob's favorite son, Joseph (Genesis 37-50), went through many evil and unfair situations. These events were not his fault. Like others, he could have been full of insecurity, cruelty, and revenge.

Instead, Joseph saw the whole picture from God's point of view. Upon being reunited with his selfish brothers, he said, "And as for you, you meant evil against me, but God meant it for good in order to bring about this present result, to preserve many people alive." (Genesis 50:20).

How could Joseph look at life in this way? Was he some kind of machine, possessing no feelings? Where did he get the courage and perspective to tell his brothers these things? The answer is given in Genesis 39:2,21, "... the LORD was with Joseph." The presence of God provided the security through the trials in addition to after the trials. Joseph knew that God had a purpose in the trials and tests. Notice that Joseph mentions that God's purpose was to "bring about this present result." Joseph refused to live in the past. He left the bitter experiences in order to live in the present.

We who believe upon Christ as Savior, have had evil and disappointing experiences. God was and is using these experiences to mold our lives into people who would humbly trust Him. Each one of us has had different obstacles to face. In all these obstacles, trials, and tests, the devil would have us to fail. In some of them, we did fail. In others, we were victorious. Satan, and some people, meant them for evil. God meant them for good.

All things, good or evil, pleasurable or uncomfortable, are for our good and for God's glory (Romans 8:28). God brings us to the present place in our lives and says, "Now, take what you have learned and be the kind of person I want you to be *today!* I have meant it all for good" (My Paraphrase).

Our family background is a teaching ground. If we learn from God's perspective, we will be secure and joyful. If we see it only as a means of disappointment, we will be insecure, bitter, fearful, and sorrowful. Regardless of age or ability, we have a choice to make: 1) We can choose to live life victoriously with the Lord right now. 2) We can choose to live life with our past trials and tests as the unreliable and depressing standard by which we measure everything.

Employment and the Pressures of Possessions

To say that the job market is very competitive would be an understatement. Work related stress abounds everywhere. Fear of being unemployed is a constant concern throughout our society. No one is exempt. Even large corporations may go bankrupt or may be taken over and sold within a moment's notice. Pressure is put upon employees to produce beyond what they accomplished in previous months or years. Unions try to take some of the anxiety away by providing a united front in negotiating salaries and benefits. The burdens on the job front continue.

The source of undue pressure and anxiety is not the place of employment. The source is the heart of man. He has a different god than the One in the Bible. His god is covetousness and greed. Colossians 3:5 equates covetousness and greed to idolatry. People worship the act of possessing things. Amassing possessions is a contest in which our society competes.

People live as though they actually believe that physical possessions is their source of security. Christ spoke of the foolishness of having possessions as one's security in Luke 12:16-21:

And He told them a parable, saying, "The land of a certain rich man was very productive. And he began reasoning to himself, saying, 'What shall I do, since I have no place to store my crops?' And he said, 'This is what I will do: I will tear down my barns and build larger ones, and there I will store all my grain and my goods. And I will say to my soul, "Soul, you have many goods laid up for many years to come; take your ease, eat, drink and be merry."' But God said to him, 'You fool! This very night your soul is required of you; and now who will own what you have prepared?' So is the man who lays up treasure for himself, and is not rich toward God."

From this outlook, insecurity is inevitable. Two obvious reasons are cited. First, this foundation is idolatrous: another god has been chosen to replace the Only God. Second, this foundation is not eternal. Viewing possessions as a foundation is clearly a basis for insecurity. Why? Temporary foundations always result in insecure structures! In this case, the result will be insecure lives. I John 2:15-17 testifies of the temporary nature of the world and of possessions:

"Do not love the world, nor the things in the world. If anyone loves the world, the love of the Father is not in him. For all that is in the world, the lust of the flesh and the lust of the eyes and the boastful pride of life, is not from the Father, but is from the world. And the world is passing away, and also its lusts; but the one who does the will of God abides forever."

The previously mentioned pressure is called the American Dream. Actually, the dream is a nightmare. The downward trend of covetousness becomes stronger and stronger. Man becomes its slave. He has to have, and if he fails to get, he trespasses beyond morals and ethics to obtain.

"What is the source of quarrels and conflicts among you? Is not the source your pleasures that wage war in your members? You lust and do not have; so you commit murder. And you are envious and cannot obtain; so you fight and quarrel. You do not have because you do not ask." James 4:1,2

The workplace becomes a place of confrontation and competition. It seems as if someone is always trying to take away the things of someone else. Pay increases and promotions are fought for at any cost. The sacrifice of integrity and honor becomes small in comparison to the need to satisfy temporary lusts. Hatred, jealousy, and strife become commonplace.

The same answer is necessary to relieve these anxieties. *Trust God!* All of man's conniving cannot feed him, clothe him, make him healthy, nor add years to his life. *Daily provisions from God are as much a miracle as the parting of the Red Sea.* The believer has no need to enter into unethical practices. He has a supernatural God Who provides all things.

One expression of poverty is, "I didn't know where my next meal was coming from." Does anyone *really know* where his next meal is coming from? Wealthy or poverty-stricken, man does not have this knowledge. He may plan that it will come out of the freezer, off the barbecue, or from a fast-food restaurant. However, the freezer may quit, the neighbor's dog may steal the burgers from the grill, or the restaurant may shut down. Only the one who is trusting the Lord knows that God will provide for all his needs.

The Bible teaches that man is to provide for his family. He is to work diligently. He is to be honest, forthright, and kind in the process. Man is to realize that all of his work and labor are under Divine Providence. Without God giving daily strength and wisdom, he is a completely helpless creature.

With these truths in mind, people can confidently and positively face their colleagues and employers. The security of knowing God's providence in all things will determine how they treat others at the workplace.

How can one have the peaceful knowledge that God will provide? *The basis for this faith is in what God has already provided.* The Lord has already provided and given eternal life to the believer in Christ. Romans 8:32 says, "He who did not spare His own Son, but delivered Him up for us all, how will He not also with Him freely give us all things?" Since God has delivered on His greatest promises of forgiveness and eternal life, there is no room for doubt. He will deliver on His promise to supply all the temporal needs of the believer (Philippians 4:19). Otherwise, the integrity of God and His Word have been compromised.

Freedom from ungodly competition is the result for all those who are secure in the Lord. They can be at peace with the Lord, knowing that all is well, because all is going to be well. They have the security of knowing that God is going to provide.

Peer Relationships

Isn't it great to see children grow up? My wife and I have had the joy of watching all four of our children grow from childhood, through adolescence, and into adulthood. Each one matured differently. Each one matured at different ages. Looking back on the experience, we say that it was fun. Going through it was indeed a struggle. My wife and I learned some maturity through the process of teaching maturity (and we are still learning). As youngsters develop into mature adults, it is interesting to see how they deal with peer pressure.

These steps of maturity are nothing new in the world of psychology. Neither are they anti-biblical. First Corinthians 13:11 says, "When I was a child, I used to speak as a child, think as a child, reason as a child; when I became a man, I did away with childish things." Godly love (I Corinthians 13) is the expression of the mature Christian. Love is also the expression of a mature adult. Secure adults are able to freely love others sincerely. Insecure adults have not graduated from their selfish childhood desires.

Generally, children get their identity and their security from their parents. Their comments are: "Mom says this." "Dad did that." "I went to the beach with my parents." "We all built a big dog house." They have no problem with belonging to and identifying with the family. Children naturally look to their parents and family for their security.

Then, the pre-teen and teenage years begin. They begin to feel pressured to be like their peers. Identity moves from parents to friends. During these years, they become people that we as parents do not know. We ask, "Could this be my son or my daughter?" It is as though they turn into completely different people. If it isn't for an occasional need, they have no reason to talk to us. Many of the things that they think, say, and do, reflect their friends' attitudes and behavior. During this period of growth they do their best *not* to be like their parents.

Finally, on the other side of adolescence emerges the mature adult. They have their own identity now. Their self-worth is based upon who they are in Christ, rather than upon what their friends think they ought to be. They do not have to be at their friend's house, locked in the bedroom, playing video games until 2:00 AM. They do not have to stick their tongue out while going up for a lay-up shot on the basketball court. They don't have to sit in a corner away from others, whispering and giggling with a friend. Those things have passed. They have put away childish things.

However, if the security of the Lord is not developed in our children's lives, they will not be exempt from continued peer pressure. Their self-worth will not be found in how God sees them in Christ. The basis of their lives will not be the Lord Jesus Christ, the One and Only True Foundation. The only recourse they have would be to gain their security from the opinions of others. Peer pressure continues to drive them to do the things that others desire. Their whole purpose in life is to be accepted by someone.

Security comes by knowing we are accepted by God. When we know that God accepts us, we know that we are safe and secure. As Christians, we do not have to lose our identity. We do not have to become slaves of someone else's opinions and desires. Romans 8:15 tells us, "For you have not received a spirit of slavery leading to fear again, but you have received a spirit of adoption as sons by which we cry out, 'Abba! Father!'" We are God's mature adult sons, set free to develop our responsibilities as He would lead us.

The insecurity brought about by peer pressure is dangerous in all relationships. The most volatile is marriage. Husbands or wives who have never become secure in the Lord, may be leaning upon the acceptance of their spouses for their security.

The Bible teaches that husbands and wives *are* to accept one another. However, if their self-worth is dependent upon their spouse's acceptance, the marriage may be insecure. It may not be truly based upon acceptance of the real person. It is based upon the acceptance of what that spouse has been pressured to become. As time passes one or both spouses tire of being someone that they are really not. They become weary of the hypocrisy. He or she decides to just be themselves. If this "new" person is rejected by the other spouse, the marriage can be destroyed.

Marriages can also be jeopardized because one can become tired of being the "daddy" or the "mommy" to the other insecure spouse. The more secure spouse may wish that the person they married would mature, "grow up," or just stop seeking constant approval. The insecure marriage partner is constantly in need of being accepted by the other partner. This unending approval-seeking process can be a drain upon any relationship, but especially a marriage. When approval is not given, the insecure spouse may look elsewhere for acceptance. If they do not look to the Lord for this acceptance, the trend continues.

Unfortunately, peer pressure is not just a teenage issue. It affects all who do not have security in the Lord. The Bible calls peer pressure the pride of life (First John 2:16). Everyone wants others to think well of them. Insecurity causes this desire to become a ruling desire, or a lust. A position at work, an educational degree, or any other accomplishment or activity can be the result of peer pressure.

Insecure, approval-seeking people may think thus: "Look at me. See what I have done. Don't you love me and accept me for what I have done?"

Jesus Christ never has accepted us on the basis of what *we* have done. However, He has completely accepted us on the basis of what *He* has done on our behalf. Being accepted by God through Christ is the only way out of peer pressure. In Christ, God thinks well of us. He has no other agenda but to bless us according to *His* will.

Summary

Our relationships are constantly being challenged by insecurities. Marriage, family, home, employment, and friendships are all affected by our relationship with God in Christ. If we are not at peace with the Lord, we will not be at peace with people. We will then continue to have improper relationships with people. Our unbalanced desire to be accepted in life will dominate all our relationships.

When our lives are filled with ourselves (and with our needs as we perceive them), we will be controlled by the emptiness of our own poverty stricken souls. Only Christ can fill the emptiness of our lives. When our lives become filled with Him, our personalities become pleasant. He has accepted us. We can build secure lives and relationships based upon *His* love for us and *His* acceptance of us. Then we will be free to be ourselves!

Chapter 14

Peace In The Local Church

God has a place where people go, a place so blessed and so serene.
It is His church, His body - a place where all may go and lean.
On one another and on the Lord - Away from the anxiety and fear,
To be built up upon the Lord - Knowing that God is always near.

People have often wondered why there are so many divisions, factions, cliques, and splits in local churches. We ignore most of the real problems by pursuing a route of "political correctness." We say, "Mrs. Jones left the church because of personality problems." In fact, this is likely only one of several churches she has left in recent years.

While dealing with this topic, it must be stated that there are legitimate biblical reasons why believers are to separate from other believers. False doctrine, unruly behavior, and immorality are not to be tolerated within the local church. However, severing the ties of most church relationships is not based upon any of these legitimate biblical reasons.

A multitude of difficulties are blamed on the issue of the "dreaded" personality. However, *every* individual has his own personality. Each believer is a member of the body of Christ. This multiple-faceted body (the church) is to function smoothly *because* of different personalities. These differences are designed to balance the church's ministries into completeness (First Corinthians 12). God's intention is to use peoples' differences to form a complete organism which would minister to everyone.

The Bible compares the body of Christ to the physical body. Romans 12:4,5 says, "For just as we have many members in one body and all the members do not have the same function, so we, who are many, are one body in Christ, and individually members one of another." Each member of the physical body differs from the other members and organs of that same body. The hand not only looks different from the foot, but also provides a different necessary function.

If we think this teaching is too basic, let us read carefully the Word of God in I Corinthians 12:12-18:

"For even as the body is one and yet has many members, and all the members of the body, though they are many, are one body, so also is Christ. For by one Spirit we were all baptized into one body, whether Jews or Greeks, whether slaves or free, and we were all made to drink of one Spirit. For the body is not one member, but many. If the foot should say, 'Because I am not a hand, I am not a part of the body,' it is not for this reason any the less a part of the body. And if the ear should say, 'Because I am not an eye, I am not a part of the body,' it is not for this reason any the less a part of the body. If the whole body were an eye, where would the hearing be? If the whole were hearing, where would the sense of smell be? But now God has placed the members, each one of them, in the body, just as He desired."

Jealousy against other church members regarding what they have and what they do in the church is not a personality problem. It is a *sin* problem! The local church is a group of believers assembled together as a volunteer army. Each soldier has his own personality. Each soldier is yet in the flesh. Fleshly sin is a catalyst used by some Christians to bring the pain and devastation of discord into the church.

Four pillars of truth need to be addressed regarding the approach to solve these problems. The first is the transformation of the Christian personality. The second is submission, which is the foundation of church unity. The third is the glorification of the Lord Jesus Christ. The fourth pillar is the leadership within the local church.

The Transformation of the Christian Personality

The death of Christ on the cross secured our souls in glory forever. This is a wonderful and beautiful truth we previously viewed in the first few chapters of this study. In addition, the death of Christ accomplished forgiveness and cleansing for us. This means that we are not going to be the same people that we were before we were saved (II Corinthians 5:17). Not only are we new creatures in God's sight, but the fundamental change of being redeemed affects our whole lifestyle. The New Testament reminds us to make our lifestyle conform to what God has made us in Christ. Philippians 2:12 says, "So then, my beloved, just as you have always obeyed, not as in my presence only, but now much more in my absence, work out your salvation with fear and trembling."

After we are saved, God is fully *expecting* our personalities to change. If our personalities do not change, they become deity to us. In Malachi 3:6, God says, "For I, the Lord, do not change; therefore you, O sons of Jacob, are not consumed." God is the only One Who does not change. Immutability (changelessness) is one of the incommunicable attributes of God. This means that God does not share this attribute with man. If we take this attribute that is exclusively God's to be ours, we claim equality with God. This is utter blasphemy.

Christ died for sinful man. This would also include man's sinful personality. We need to bring our personalities to the Lord so that He may mold them into what pleases Him. How do we know what kind of people we are to be? Are hatred, anxiety, unruliness, unkindness, pride, impatience, and unfaithfulness sin? The Bible very graphically says, "Yes!"

Is gentleness a personality trait? Are love, joy, and peace traits which affect our personalities? Will self-control help us to be able to get along with other people? Will faithfulness help to develop trustworthy Christian friendships? Will God use patience and meekness as He molds our personalities? Yes! Yes! Yes! The Holy Spirit is constantly working upon our personalities to bring forth these godly changes. Having personalities that are controlled by the Holy Spirit is essential for sound relationships within the local church.

As discussed previously, the fruit of the Holy Spirit is hindered by insecurity. Therefore, insecurity is the basis for "personality problems" within the local church. Christians can tenaciously cling to ungodly ways as a result of not yielding themselves to the Word of God and to the Holy Spirit. They hold on to these insecurities firmly. As a result, they have not given themselves any other alternative. They must use their personalities as excuses to sin against other Christians and against God.

Submission

The second pillar of truth that has been neglected by believers is submission. Ephesians 5:18-21 tells the plan of God for filling believers with His Holy Spirit:

"And do not get drunk with wine, for that is dissipation, but be filled with the Spirit, speaking to one another in psalms and hymns and spiritual songs, singing and making melody with your heart to the Lord; always giving thanks for all things in the name of our Lord Jesus Christ to God, even the Father; *and be subject to one another* in the fear of Christ. (italics -- mine).

One of the major results of the Holy Spirit's filling of the believer is the sweet testimony of submission. Verse 21 makes this very clear.

How can we possibly be subject to one another? Christians are so imperfect. They are too much -- like us! Why would we want to give them the opportunity to mess up our lives? We can pay our tithes. We can share Christ by witnessing to others. We can teach Sunday School classes. We can organize church functions. We can sing in the choir, work in the nursery, etc. We can be in charge of any or all of these ministries. But, we still may not get along with others. We may not trust others. We may insist on having things our own way.

Only believers who are secure in the Lord will be able to submit themselves to other believers. Without being secure in the Lord, other Christians can appear to be a threat. Insecurity will cause the believer's grip to tighten on what he has and what he wants. Security will cause him to be free to let go of his own ways. Why? He is going to trust the Lord. He will do this in the "fear of Christ." He is going to trust Christ's ability rather than his own ability. Submission to others looks as if it is an act of trusting others. For the Spirit-filled believer, it is an act of trusting the Lord.

When this security of submission takes place, believers begin to work as God intended the body of Christ to function. In unity, they will esteem others better than themselves. They will not think more highly of themselves than they ought to think. Other Christians' desires and needs will become more important than their own needs. All factions, cliques, "personality differences," and divisions will quickly vanish.

Satan hates a united church. He will bring fear and insecurity into the assembly any way he possibly can. He knows that Spirit-filled Christians, submitting themselves to one another, are a great danger to his kingdom. Most of the issues that the devil uses to accomplish division are without any substance: the color of the church carpet, who is allowed in the nursery, who sings in the choir, etc. It is interesting that believers don't fight over who has the delight of cleaning the church toilets!

Well-grounded Christians who are trusting the Lord and submitting to Him are keys to Satan's defeat. As they submit to Jesus Christ they gain security from the Lord to submit to one another. Great unity in the body of Christ will then be experienced in the local church.

Glorifying the Lord Jesus Christ

Church unity is also compromised when the leadership of the church does not emphasize the Lord Jesus Christ. Colossians 1:18 tells us that Christ is the head of the church. The primary emphasis of each individual is to be upward. Contrary to the world's standards, it is not to be primarily inward, nor outward. The purpose of the local church is to glorify the Lord. How can this be done?

Remember, the church is made up of individuals. Each individual member of the local congregation should have the glory of God as his or her personal agenda (I Corinthians 10:31). When this occurs, the unity of the church is safe. When this does not occur, the unity of the church is in jeopardy. Other lesser causes soon cloud the skies when Jesus Christ ceases to be the focal point of the individuals who make up the congregation.

If I am insecure, I will be more interested in glorifying myself than I will be in glorifying the Lord. When this happens, I *must* have my own way. I will feel threatened by others even if they are trying to live for the Lord. Many churches have been split or have lost members because of this very carnal outlook in life.

Each person of the church is to direct his or her emphasis toward the Lord, to glorify Him. This common goal will bring unity. "Personality" conflicts and strife will then cease to exist.

A happy day is expected for us as we wait for the redemption of the body! Heaven will be the place where we will experience the perfect unity we long for. The flesh will no longer hinder us in our fellowship with the Lord and with one another.

Church Leadership

It is common for church leaders to by-pass proper Biblical leadership in order to establish unity. They do this by diminishing the responsibilities of the members. This has been accomplished in one of two ways.

The first way is for the leaders of the church to give members "non-spiritual" responsibilities. The members are given tasks that keep them busy. They take care of the physical church properties, they give their money, they work in the nursery, they prepare dinners, and they attend services. All during this process, they are told that they are serving the Lord. They feel more spiritual as they become busier. When they have a problem they are to go directly to the pastor. He, in turn, will try to give the solution to their problem.

The intention is to keep people so busy that they do not have time to argue with other members. They are so busy "serving the Lord" that they don't have opportunity to bless or curse their fellow members.

The second way that member responsibility is diminished is far more common. It is done through the elevation of the authority of the leadership of the church. Pastors become dictators and deacons become church boards. Where this cannot be done, an extra group is established called "elders" or some other name. Church members are not allowed to be involved in the decision making process. The leadership of the church may refuse to be embarrassed by dealing with the hassles of people who might not agree. Those in authority maintain that the opportunity to disagree is never to be given to "irresponsible members."

In Revelation 2:6,15, God tells His churches that He hates the deeds and doctrines of the Nicolaitans. The name "Nicolaitans" is from two Greek words which mean "conquer" and "people." If the Nicolaitans were true to their name, they would be called "people conquerors." It is no wonder that God hates this teaching! His intention was and always has been to present His Son as the only Lord over His people. At times, church leaders have become guilty of becoming "little popes" over the flock of God.

Such domineering attitudes from church leaders can be caused by their own insecurities. Their lack of trusting the Lord causes them to become "success oriented." *They seemed to have forgotten that true success for every believer is simply "trusting the Lord."* The work and labor that comes from trusting God is always a manifestation of the character of God. Therefore, such work is kind, firm, peaceful, and loving. Leaders desperately need to trust the Lord, so that they might exhibit these characteristics. A church leader who is trusting God will allow the Lord to move upon the hearts of their congregations as He sees fit.

Both of these methods of diminishing member responsibility have been very successful in churches today. However, both methods are wrong. Both methods are concerned with marketing the church with the appearance of success. Marketing the church has become more popular than dealing with the basic problems of individual believers. If the church can appear to the world as a church that has no problems, it is looked upon as a "good" church. A "good" church is therefore "marketable" to the world. Such a church has merely covered or ignored its problems.

By following the authoritarian leadership of men, the church may set aside the headship and the preeminence of the Lord Jesus Christ. The headship of Jesus Christ may be preached, without being practiced. The insecurity of church leaders may have caused them to usurp the authority of Christ. God *hates* this!

The idea behind these approaches may be to make the church run more smoothly and more efficiently. This is a noble desire. However, it is never good to apply an unbiblical and ungodly means to accomplish a good desire. Abraham found that out when he took Sarah's handmaid to be his wife (Genesis 16-21). The outcome of that "noble" desire led to catastrophe.

People who are leaders in the church have certain God-given qualities and gifts. These qualities are to help them to perform their functions of leadership to the church. These God-given qualities are not intended to be used as tools to usurp the authority of Christ over the members. Nor, is it intended for church leaders to be the only ones who are held accountable for the ministry of a particular church. Diminishing member authority also gives the perception of diminished member responsibility.

Members of most congregations understand the relationship between authority and responsibility. People are willing to give all the authority to the church leaders. They know very well that whoever has the *authority* also has the *responsibility* to perform the work of the ministry. This may sound like an easy solution for church members. However, all Christians are *still* responsible to the Lord Jesus Christ for the ministry of the church. Jesus Christ does not cease to be the head of the church just because some leaders have become domineering dictators.

The proper way to bring unity is to teach that each member is responsible to the Lord Jesus Christ, the only true authority over the local church. Each member is just as accountable to Christ as a pastor, a Bible school teacher, a deacon, or a missionary. Each member has particular functions to fulfill. While each member does not perform the same responsibilities of the leadership, each one is equally responsible to God. Each one needs to be encouraged to be responsible to take his God-given position in the local church before the Lord. God's intended result is to have an efficient organism functioning in unity. This efficient organism is to function so as to bring glory to the Lord Jesus Christ (Ephesians 2:21,22).

Summary

Just as in our families, so also our relationships within the local church are affected by our own personal relationships with the Lord. Our personalities, our submission to one another, the glorification of Christ, and responsible church leadership are all affected by us as individuals. When we do not take our proper place before the Lord, the body of Christ is adversely affected.

However, when we believe God and trust in Him, the threatening and competing characteristics within the local church cease to exist. When this happens, the body of Christ takes on the peaceful attractive security that glorifies the Lord in love and unity.

Conclusion

(Steps to Becoming Secure in Christ)

Security causes freedom and freedom expresses security. If you are secure, you will be free to be yourself as the Lord has planned. If you have been set free from your sins, you will be able to walk securely with God.

The following is a formula or process for becoming secure in the Lord Jesus Christ. The plan is simple and it is based on faith. Remember, simplicity is not always synonymous with ease. Speaking the plan, writing the plan, reading the plan, and understanding the plan are not the same as living the plan. There are six simple steps necessary to gain this walk of spiritual freedom and security.

1) Know Christ As Savior

Matthew 1:21 tells us, "And she shall bear a Son; and you shall call His name Jesus, for it is He who will save His people from their sins." Jesus Christ is to be known as He is, the Savior. The Scriptural definition of Christ as Savior is: He came to be the deliverer of His people from their sins.

Sin always brings guilt. Guilt is characterized by

confusion and insecurity. Delivering us from our sins will therefore deliver us from our guilt. Forgiveness and eternal life are the products of this great deliverance. Forgiveness and eternal life are words of security. The reception of forgiveness results in joy. The possession of eternal life results in peace. Sin and guilt are words of insecurity. Sin results in death, or separation from God. Guilt results in confusion, anger, and depression.

One must believe that Christ paid the full penalty of his sins on the cross of Calvary. This is the only way that one can be rid of the insecurities and confusion caused by sin. One must realize that Jesus Christ alone is the Perfect Lamb of God, slain for his sins. Jesus personally took man's punishment upon Himself. It is Christ's death on the cross that God accepts as the perfect sacrifice for man's sins (II Corinthians 5:21). Then, and only then, can people walk in the joy and freedom of forgiveness and eternal life (Romans 6:23; Romans 10:9,10,13).

2) Trust Christ as Lord

Is Jesus Christ the Lord of your life? If you have received Him as your personal Savior, you received the Lord. Acts 10:31 tells us to believe on the "*Lord* Jesus Christ." Colossians 2:6 says, "As you therefore have received Christ Jesus the *Lord*..." (italics -- mine).

He has been and always will be the Master. The problem that we have is that we fail to recognize His Lordship in all things. A daily walk of trust under His leadership is essential for security. Proverbs 3:5,6 are great verses of trust: "Trust in the LORD with all your heart, And do not lean on your own understanding. In all your ways acknowledge Him, And He will make your paths straight."

Straight paths from the Lord are secure paths. They are not filled with twists, turns, and obstacles. God's paths are paths of safety.

This is intensely practical. Submission was discussed in the previous chapter on the local church. However, submission is not possible unless there is an authority to which one is to submit. Jesus Christ *is* that Authority. Building lives upon Him as the believers' foundation develops the practical path of security.

3) Experience Christ as Friend

Having Jesus Christ as our Friend is a unique situation for us. We have no friend like this on earth. No person is looked upon as our closest friend and also our most authoritative boss at the same time. On earth, the two do not seem to mix together. This is exactly Who Jesus Christ is: Friend and Lord.

Jesus Christ was here on this earth. He knows trials and tests. He even knows death. He was "...tempted in all things as we are, yet without sin" (Hebrews 4:15). He has experienced what we go through. He knows us deeply and completely, yet He still loves us. He will never leave us nor will He ever allow us to depart from Him.

I am convinced that my responsibility as a servant of God is to try to convince people of one great truth: "Jesus Christ really loves them." It is important that we believe that Jesus Christ really loves us as much as He says He does. This is called grace. He loves us even though we do not deserve, nor have we ever deserved His love. His love to us remains constant, emanating from the heart of God (Romans 8:31-39).

We are stubborn and proud. We do not want to be obligated by the love of Christ; neither do we want to admit that we need His love. We are strange characters. We would rather be beaten into submission than to be loved into submission. When we are beaten, we feel that we have already paid our debt. When we receive infinite love, we know we are infinitely obligated.

Accept the friendship of Christ today. Walk with Him. Do not be afraid of Him. Trust Him. He will not hurt you. Always be in fellowship with Him by remembering that He died for you. He's your friend.

4) Realize that God is Sovereign

God is in charge and He knows what He is doing. We might not know what He is doing. However, we know that what He is doing is always good. We know that the goodness of God is for our benefit and blessing. Whatever the trials or the tests, God is always good.

After I received Christ as my Savior, I began to live the new life that God had given to me. I did not struggle with the assurance of my salvation. However, I did wonder why God had allowed evil circumstances to be a part of my life as a child and teenager. It was not until I was a young pastor that I realized and accepted that it was all the plan of God. He had led me through the path that was very humbling. As I trust the Lord, I am able to live without bitterness today. The humility caused by evil has always been with me. I am greatly humbled by knowing the weakness and degradation which is caused by sin.

Satan hates humility. God loves humility. For, it is then that His sufficient grace brings the greatest glory to Himself. It also brings the greatest joy to the believer.

5) Believe the Word of God

James 1:21 tells of the great power of the Word of God. It is powerful enough to save our souls. Therefore, it is powerful enough for us to live by. It is to be authoritatively active in our lives. Hebrews 4:12 also tells of the great effective power of God's Word.

The Bible is to be the source of our victory. It is to enable us to be the kind of people that God wants us to be. We are to be rooted and established in the Holy Word of God. We are to be growing by the nourishment from the Scriptures (I Peter 2:2).

Our faithful acceptance of the Scriptures is vital to our fellowship with the Lord Jesus Christ. Jesus taught that the Word of God would keep us clean as we would abide (fellowship) in Him (John 15:3). Being rooted in Him (the Word of God) will give us the stability that we need to grow and bear fruit. Jesus wants us to bear much fruit. A fruitful person is also a joyful person.

Often, we do not want to believe and receive the Word of God. We have excuses: too busy, too tired, too boring, too irrelevant, too difficult, etc. This is unfortunate. This step toward security is of utmost importance. It is also one of the steps that the Christian casts aside most quickly. Romans 10:17 tells that faith is the product of the Word of God. We have proven from the Scriptures that faith is essential for our eternal and temporal security.

6) Manifest a Life of Faith

We have now gone full circle and have returned to where we began. Faith in Christ as our Savior is where we started. Faith that grows as we are established in His Word is the path we are to tread. This is the goal. The process is the goal and the goal is the process: faith.

Faith must *never* be an abstract concept for the believer. Faith is to be as genuine, vibrant, and as effective as God Himself is. Faith is the avenue that God has chosen through which to represent Himself to people. He does this through those who believe. If our faith does not give a true representation of God, we must question our faith's location. Is our faith truly in God through His Word? Or, has our faith been placed in an inferior object? Have we started to trust ourselves again? Have we placed our faith in circumstances? Have we lost sight of the awesome omnipotence of our Sovereign God?

Faith in God through the Word of God is to be the rule that governs our entire lives. Without it, we will not obey the Lord. Without it, God will not be pleased. Without it, we will not be secure. With faith in God, we will ride through all the storms of life successfully. We will trust God's sovereign hand in all things. We will stop trusting ourselves and our circumstances.

Faith is directly related to our relationships with God and with mankind. Faith in God causes us to see all of life from the peaceful, secure point of view that God desires for us. First, we will live peacefully with God. Second, we will be at peace within ourselves. Third, we will handle all our circumstances peacefully. Finally, we will be able to live peaceably with people.

Faith in God through Christ begins our lives anew. It nourishes us along the way. And it assures us of our glorious future in heaven forever.

While faith is necessary for our security, it would be well for us to remember Who we are to be trusting. The Object of our faith is the Lord Jesus Christ. He is all powerful. He is full of grace and truth. He is all wise. He is infinitely compassionate.

Epilogue

Jesus Christ is the Truth (John 14:6). The Truth will set you free (John 8:32). That which is not from God is not true. That which is false will only lead into bondage. You can be free to be yourself. You do not have to be poured into another person's mold. You do not have to be weak or fearful. You do not have to be poured into the world's mold. You do not have to be a slave to someone else's ideas. You do not have to be in bondage to the desires of the flesh. You do not have to rule and dominate people and situations.

You really can be happy in life. It is not a myth. It is not an abstract theory without substance. You can have the full, abundant life that Jesus promised in John 10:10. It is a life of love, steadfastness, and forgiveness. The foundation of this life is Christ. The entrance into this secure life is Christ. The building of this life of freedom and security is to be founded upon Christ. The result in eternity is the eternal presence of Christ. Let us determine to walk with the Lord by faith in His Word, thus becoming peaceful, happy, and secure.

Faith in God through the Lord Jesus Christ is our only basis for security and freedom. We cannot obtain a secure and free lifestyle from any other source. Security is not found in material things, employment, family, education, entertainment, or religion. It is found in the Lord Jesus Christ. The secure, practical lifestyle with Christ ought to be the goal of all Christians. May God be glorified as believers pursue that goal and live in freedom and security!

Free To Be Me can be used as a devotional or Bible study guide, or in Bible and theology classes. It makes a great gift for anyone interested in developing a secure relationship with God. It also can be used for evangelism and discipleship. Order from:

**Beacon Light Publishing, Inc.
P.O. Box 1612
Thousand Oaks, CA 91358
Phone: (805) 583-2002**

1-5 copies $9.95 each   Include $2.50 shipping and hand-
6-10 copies $8.95 each   ling for the first book plus 75 cents
11-15 copies $7.95 each   for each additional book ordered
16 + copies $7.00 each   on the same form.

* *

ORDER FORM

Your Name: _____

Address: _____

City, State: _____

Zip code: _____ Ph: (____) _____

Number of copies ___ X above price: _____

CA orders add 8.25% sales tax: _____

Shipping and Handling: _____

Total enclosed: _____

Please include check or money order payable to **Beacon Light Publishing, Inc.** Indicate how many copies you are ordering. Include the shipping and handling fee with your payment. Do not sent cash. Allow 2 weeks for delivery.

Free To Be Me can be used as a devotional or Bible study guide, or in Bible and theology classes. It makes a great gift for anyone interested in developing a secure relationship with God. It also can be used for evangelism and discipleship. Order from:

Beacon Light Publishing, Inc.
P.O. Box 1612
Thousand Oaks, CA 91358
Phone: (805) 583-2002

1-5 copies	$9.95 each	Include $2.50 shipping and hand-
6-10 copies	$8.95 each	ling for the first book plus 75 cents
11-15 copies	$7.95 each	for each additional book ordered
16 + copies	$7.00 each	on the same form.

* *

<u>ORDER FORM</u>

Your Name: _____

Address: _____

City, State: _____

Zip code: _____ Ph: (____) _____

Number of copies ___ X above price: _____

CA orders add 8.25% sales tax: _____

Shipping and Handling: _____

Total enclosed: _____

Please include check or money order payable to **Beacon Light Publishing, Inc.** Indicate how many copies you are ordering. Include the shipping and handling fee with your payment. Do not sent cash. Allow 2 weeks for delivery.